To my special, wonderful [...]

Reg

Spirituality for Scientists and Engineers

A Travel Guide

Reginald Hamer

Copyright © 2017 Reginald Hamer

ISBN-13: 978-0692921920
ISBN-10: 0692921923
Library of Congress Control Number: 2018900513

Logos Today, Campbell, CA.

Science and Religion, Self-Help, Spirituality, Science

Front cover artwork: Tjdatsrt, DSC_8338, Chambered Nautilus, Flickr, Creative Commons

Front cover design: Mark Hamer Back cover artwork: "Tide Comes In", by Richard, Fort Clonque, Alderney, Flicker Creative Commons

Back cover design: Mark Hamer

Author photograph by Life Touch Studios

A Journey Begins

Be patient towards all that is unsolved in your heart
and try to love the questions themselves,
like locked rooms and like books
that are now written in a foreign tongue.
Do not seek the answers which cannot be given you
because you would not be able to live them.
And the point is to live everything.
Live the questions now.
Perhaps you will then gradually, without noticing it,
live along some distant day into the answer.
—Rainer Maria Rilke

Contents

Introduction   **V**

Introduction

If you have a technical education, you may not realize it, but you are straddling two worlds all the time. You have to alternate between the world of science and the world of human concerns. These two worlds have different perceptions, values, needs, and priorities. Our formal education prepared us for technical work but could have left us far short of being comfortable in the human and spiritual worlds!

The purpose of this book is to help you become aware of the challenges which face all technically trained people. The book will provide tools and insights that can help us to continue in our search for wholeness in our lives in order to help us find a fuller, more abundant, more aware, and more appreciative life. It will also show us how to have a greater vision, feel more at home, possess a greater ability to enjoy life, and be able to relate to others in meaningful, loving relations.

> The glory of God is a man/woman
> who is fully alive!
> —Irenaeus

Background

This book is based on my many years of reading scholarly books of science and religion, plus reflecting on my own life experience in trying to make sense of my spiritual life together with my training in science. My results are based on several decades of research in the fields of science, history of science, philosophy, philosophy of science, theology, and psychology, as well as studies in science and religion. I was primarily motivated by my own struggles to reconcile my human-lived experience with my heavy technical training as I raised a family and searched for spiritual values in my life.

I have broken the book up with short, easy-to-scan subheadings so it can be browsed comfortably. Feel free to scan through the chapters, pausing at a particular subheading that might catch your attention.

It is not my intent to create a dichotomy between science and religion, but rather to cherish them both by showing their common ground, while spelling out their unique separate contributions to our life endeavors.

This is not meant to be a heavy-handed academic work that carefully spells out all the minute, intricate nuances of an issue. I've made a concerted effort to present every subject in its absolutely simplest form, just enough to get the idea across. I have made an effort to avoid jargon. If a technical term is essential to my expressing a point, I have included definitions and examples as needed. If you want more detailed coverage of a particular topic, please refer to the bibliographies at the end of each chapter. The end of each chapter also includes suggestions to help you summarize or put into action what was presented there.

For scientists: even though the chapters do not need to be read in any fixed order, it's important to include the chapter on language at some point, preferably early on.

For my nontechnical readers: I will occasionally illustrate a concept by providing an example from engineering or physics. If you're not a person with a science background, please don't feel intimidated; you can just skip over these examples and move right along.

My Intended Audience

This book is written for all people who are earnestly searching for spiritual values in their lives. I have specifically directed this book to the technically trained: scientists, engineers, and computer programmers. Equally important, this book is intended to help their spouses or significant others to better understand their technically trained loved ones. Counselors, therapists, and ministers with strong communities of engineers in their congregations will also find this material essential.

I will share with you my own struggles and blind alleys and insights that were helpful. Chapter 2, "Important Differences in Language," and chapter 8, "Moving Forward: Obstacles to Overcome," will be particularly useful to those counseling or ministering to scientific types.

My hope is that you will be able to move forward in your spiritual search after reading this book while reflecting on how it may mirror some of your own life experience.

My Story

After graduating from engineering school, I faced a great question: If science is so great and I believe in it and I have seen so many wonderful results, why don't other people use science to solve their human problems? What is wrong with these people? Why don't they just identify the inputs and outputs and isolate the system behavior?

I had a lot to learn!

This book reflects my personal struggles to reconcile my education with my spiritual search. I hope that sharing my experiences will be useful to others in pursuing their own spiritual journeys.

We have been seriously let down by our education. In the search for excellence, excellence is bought at a great price.

The technical advances that thrill us today will be considered passé in a few years. Specialization is also an important issue. We need to look for broader and more enduring values than just technical achievement.

I was at a party once where one of the guests arrived late in a state of great excitement. He had just received the first printed copy of a book he had written on the topic of computer-chip testing. As he proudly waved his new book around for all to see, people shook their heads, applauded, and oohed and aahed, but the truth of the matter was that not one single person even bothered to open the book because no one could understand a word of it or even remotely relate to it. Excellence usually demands narrowing our allegiances to the exclusion of others. This leads to isolation.

I spent nine years as a student, studying fourteen hours a day, six and a half days a week. After finishing my schooling, I settled down to raise a family. I went through real culture shock realizing what was expected of me as a husband and father! None of my schooling had prepared me to be a husband or a parent. I had to unlearn things and learn them all over in order to survive and thrive!

Chapter Overview

The book helps sensitize us to the impact our technical education may have had on our spiritual search.

Chapter 1 gives a brief historical overview of how science came to be so powerful a force in our Western world. Knowledge of history is important because what happened at the time of the scientific revolution created a painful tear between our consciousness of the physical world and our spirituality. To understand this present separation of science and spirituality, we need to return to that era and understand it beyond the stereotypes given to us by the "infotainment" TV industry.

Chapter 2 reviews issues in the use of language. Science and spirituality have distinct languages. The first stumbling block in crossing from one field to the other is misunderstanding the language of the other side. Here, I point out the essential differences in language between these two worlds, and I give you guidelines on how to avoid getting trapped or misled by these differences.

Chapter 3 looks at the incredibly rich common foundations shared by science and spirituality. I think very few people are aware of these!

Chapter 4 reviews some important limitations of science and how they affect us. We will explore the essence of what it means to perform scientific experiments and how these methods carry or do not carry over into everyday life.

Chapter 5 looks at human development in order to more fully achieve our human potential and move forward on our spiritual journey.

Chapter 6 looks at emotions, a totally neglected area of our technical education! This chapter discusses a variety of emotions and how they can hurt or help us. We will define emotional intelligence and explore how it is an integral part of our spiritual growth. We will learn to acknowledge, value, and work alongside our emotions.

Chapter 7 shows us how a science-only culture can at times hinder our person-to-person relationships and gives us tools for achieving heart-to-heart relationships. All spiritual growth requires quality in-depth relationships with others.

Chapter 8 looks at the barriers we may run into when we make the transition from a fully technical science-only world to include and value the human world of spirituality and wholeness.

Chapter 9 is a useful presentation of a variety of spiritual paths and practices for our spiritual journey.

Chapter 10 gives a final personal reflection.

Also included in the back of the book is a list of common metaphors plus an index.

Acknowledgments

To Barb
This book would never have been written were it not for the incredible love and support I have received from my wife, Barbara Manseau Hamer. You are the sunshine of my life!

My son Mark has always been a special joy in my life. Mark gave me much-needed support plus created all of the great artwork for this book using his rich artistic talents. My son Paul (1966-1991) taught me so much about the incredible gift of being alive "Death is no dreams!" My very special daughter-in-law Michele has given me much help in researching the web plus her support. My granddaughter Ruby is a joy to my heart, she has also contributed to the illustrations in the book.

No man is an island! I am forever indebted to my larger family who have taught me their lived wisdom:

My parents, Charlie and Elsie Hamer, my grandparents, Geoff and Nellie who very generously helped to raise me in a needy, bewildering world. My grandmother Maria de la Luz who will always be an inspirational role model for me. My grand uncle, Walter Emmanuel, who believed in me and very generously enabled me to go to college in the USA. My aunt and spiritual mother, Lilian Carmen who rescued me in my childhood and brought redemption to my life. My very special in-laws, Leo and Jeannette Manseau who took me in as their son.

My doctoral thesis advisor, Dr. James Henry Mulligan Jr., who initiated me to the rigors of experimental work. I am indebted to him, among other things, for teaching me professionalism and intellectual honesty.

I received much-needed friendship and support, plus detailed proofreading insights, from Christine LoFranco Taylor, Howard Hill, Ron Murphy, Carol Reber Murphy, Steve Stolarik, Paul Hayter, Joy Andrews Hayter, Diane Mathios, Martin E. Hellman, Ken A. Souza (1943–2016), Emily Holton, Jim Davis, Brock Carpenter, Kathleen Eagan, and Burt Corsen.

My nephew, Peter Manseau, gave me warm friendship and encouragement while patiently providing me with sage advice on the intricacies of being an author.

I am deeply indebted to: Rev. William Joseph Manseau, Audrey Siebert-Nall, Hale Anderson, Jim Fisher, Ann Thompson, members of Ann Thompson's memoir class, Bob Russell, Bernie Wood, Rev. Mary Blessing, Jim Blessing, Rev. Bruce Bramlett, Ken Shuey, Rev Karen Siegfriedt, Rev. Wilma Jakobsen, Rev. John Buenz, Luis Woodhouse, Carol Clark, Richard Clark, Kathy Yates, and Bob Jurgen.

Chapter 1
The Scientific Revolution: Uncovering the Beauty

> This most beautiful system of the Sun, planets, and comets, could only proceed from the counsel and dominion of an intelligent and powerful Being.
>
> —Sir Isaac Newton

Overview

Like everybody else, I have watched many TV specials about the Galileo affair. I wanted to go beyond these mass productions to understand this complex set of events by researching several books written by world-level scholars. Conflict, setting, personalities, long-term consequences, our long-term heritage, and religion intertwined with political power and personalities interacting. Polarization, good guy versus bad guys, a win-lose conflict. The sense of triumph, superiority, and exclusivity. The ability to control nature creates power, and power can, at times, corrupt.

Science and technology permeate our modern world. They are such an integral and powerful part of our lives today that it is hard for us to picture a time when things were otherwise. In order for us to better understand our present-day values, methods, and expectations of science, we need to review the pertinent historical events that led up to our times.

The scientific revolution did not happen overnight. It required a significant series of events, the formation of institutions, and an evolution of attitudes. Let's do a quick review of the precursors to the scientific revolution.

The Legacy of the Middle Ages

According to Lindberg,

Scholars of the later Middle Ages had created a broad intellectual tradition, in the absence of which, subsequent progress in natural philosophy [what we call the physical sciences today] would have been inconceivable...They created a critical climate in which the highly-authoritative teachings of Aristotle were scrutinized, and in which its fate depended on its ability to explain observed phenomena rather than any authoritative statement it might possess. This synthesis gained an institutional home in the medieval universities. The classical tradition in natural philosophy [Physics] became one of the central elements in the curriculum encountered by everybody who embarked on higher studies. To be educated meant, by definition, to be educated in the philosophical tradition emanating from antiquity, including its natural philosophy. The scientific revolution brought about global change in the way nature was understood and in the methods used to study it (Lindberg 1992, 360–8).

The Scientific Revolution

In order for the scientific revolution to take place, some seven elements were required (Lindberg 1992, 360–8; Smethurst 1955).

First, a belief that the universe was orderly, rational, and consistent and that we could express and understand this order by use of reason, as derived from the rich rational tradition developed in classical Greece and Christian scholarship.

"Without the belief that it is possible to grasp reality with our theoretical constructions, without the belief in the inner harmony of our world, there could be no science. This belief is and always will remain the fundamental motive for all scientific creation" (Einstein and Infeld 1938).

"Faith is necessary for the scientist even to get started, because he must have confidence that there is order in the universe, and the human mind—in fact his own mind—has a good chance of understanding this order" (Townes 2013, 185).

Second, a belief in the unity of the universe. This implies that when we observe a pattern in measured data on Earth, this has the potential to apply elsewhere in the universe because of the universe's underlying unity. The first great scientist was Aristotle, who broke with polytheism to believe in one single divine mind or first cause. The Abrahamic faiths—Judaism, Christianity, and Islam—also provide this vision of unity because of their monotheistic beliefs.

Third, the existence of scholarly institutions such as the universities that had been in operation since the 1100s and had a tradition of scholarly debate based on reason, which was active all through the Middle Ages.

Fourth, mathematical tools. Algebra was developed by Muslim scholars and discovered by the West during the Renaissance. In order to describe, process, and interpret patterns occurring in experimental data, algebra was essential. Kepler found that a planet's positions could be accounted for best by making it move on an ellipse, not a circle. He also discovered the equal area law: a line drawn from the Sun to a planet sweeps out equal areas in equal times as a planet moves (Principe 2011, 58).

Fifth, instruments. Astronomy had been around for thousands of years and had reached the limits of what could be accomplished using simple, unaided human eyesight. In order to move forward, it was necessary to extend the range of the human senses. Galileo was the first one to use the recently invented telescope. The telescope gave Galileo insights into the makeup of the solar system that were impossible to arrive at using unaided human vision.

Sixth, an openness to a hands-on approach rather than pure conceptualization. Ever since the Renaissance, scholars had placed great emphasis on abstract thinking. Both Galileo and Newton broke new ground by being hands-on experimenters as well as abstract thinkers.

Seventh, the mind-set that would separate the description of physical events from their philosophical explanation. This approach was first used by both Galileo and Newton. Newton commented when he derived his law of universal attraction that he could not explain how action-at-a-distance took place, but could only describe it. Not being able to explain this effect did not stop him from going ahead with his work.

Historical Development

Our primal ancestors were aware of points of light in the dark night sky. They could identify patterns in the clusters of these points of light, patterns having an orderly west-east motion that repeated yearly. Our ancestors used these moving patterns to predict and anticipate the times for planting and harvesting seasons and the migration of herds of animals. There were some points of light, however, that did not follow this simple pattern of west-east motion but seemed to wander in loop the loop patterns.

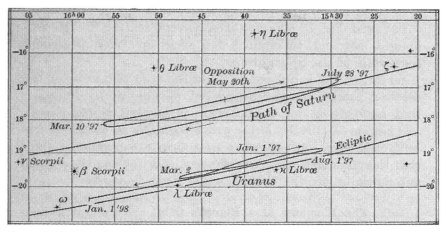

Figure 1 Planetary loop-de-loop trajectory

These bodies were named *planets*, which means "wanderers."

Precursors

The scientific revolution had many precursors:

- Claudius Ptolemy was a Greco-Egyptian mathematician and astronomer who created the first working model, a set of convenient data tables that predicted the positions and motions of the planets throughout the year. These tables worked reasonably well, becoming a standard reference that would be used by all for the next two thousand years. Over the centuries, as problems were found with Ptolemy's tables, astronomers made additions and modifications to these tables. Cumulative patches upon patches and modifications upon modifications eventually created a monstrosity.

- Pythagoras (570–495 BC) taught that numbers are embedded everywhere in the universe.

5

- Aristotle (384–322 BC), who later became the highest authority in the Renaissances, taught that all planets were located in concentric spheres around the sun.

- Aristarchus of Samos (Ca. 270 BC) was the first person known to have ever proposed a sun-centered system. Aristarchus calculated the size of Earth and measured the sizes and distances of the moon and sun in a treatise that has survived.

- Georg Rheticus (1514–1574) taught that a mathematical model for the universe had to be elegant, concise, and simple. Astronomers at that time were convinced that God would construct a harmonious and symmetrical universe, a simple universe absent superfluous, ugly details: "Should we not attribute to God, the Creator of nature, that skill which we observe in the common makers of clocks? For they carefully avoid inserting in the mechanism any superfluous wheel, or any whose function could be served better by another with a slight change of position" (Pine 1988, 132).

Accomplishments and Themes

We see two overarching themes: a passion for the truth and a response to the call of beauty, which eventually brought on a colossal thinking-outside-the-box experience as a consequence of their dogged, relentless efforts to uncover the truth. What drove the Copernican revolution were the seeds planted by the Pythagoreans two thousand years earlier, a deep conviction that the universe was orderly, mathematical, and beautiful.

As with many of our research projects, which require several sequential steps to complete, the Copernican revolution went through important stages: initial inspiration, conceptualization,

Figure 2 Nicholas Copernicus

motivation, refinement of instruments to be used, collection of data, imaginative and creative search for patterns in the data, expressing these patterns in mathematical form, summarizing the final results, and then presenting these results in an effective manner to the rest of the world. These developmental stages were carried out by Copernicus, Tycho Brahe, Kepler, Galileo, and Newton.

Nicholas Copernicus

According to Lawrence M. Principe, Copernicus spent most of his life as a canon—an administrative post in holy orders—for the cathedral church in Frauenburg, Poland. He studied canon law in Bologna and medicine in Padua and earned a doctorate in law at Ferrara in 1503.

While at Bologna, Copernicus began studying astronomy. Around 1514, he wrote an outline of his idea that the sun, not Earth, was at the center of the planetary system.

In his dedicatory letter to Pope Paul III, Copernicus referred to the Ptolemaic system, with its eccentrics, epicycles, and treatment of each planet separately as a "monster." Noting that the world is created by the best and most systematic artisan of all, he said it should be harmonious. Copernicus, as the humanist he was, saw himself as clearing away later "accretions" to return to Plato's original challenge of showing the well-ordered nature of celestial motions. Copernicus started the process by his dissatisfaction with the messiness of the Ptolemaic system. Since Copernicus was a Pythagorean, he looked for beauty, simplicity, and symmetry, which were sadly missing in the Ptolemaic system. He saw that a sun-centered system reflected that fact.

> We ascribe beauty to that which is simple; which has no superfluous parts; which exactly answers its end; which stands related to all things; which is the mean of many extremes.   Ralph Waldo Emerson

Copernicus's work circulated in manuscript and so sufficiently established his reputation as an astronomer that in 1515, when a Church council was considering how to reform the old Julian calendar—in use since the Romans and now in need of an overhaul—they wrote to ask for Copernicus's opinion. *On the Revolutions of the Heavenly Orbs* appeared in 1543 and stayed in print for more than seventy years. There was a muted response to his publication. His data did not fit any better than the old system. There were also some objections based on the experience of reality: How does Earth remain suspended without falling down to center of the universe? Also, how can Earth be moving when we have no sensation of motion? However, his tables for calculating planetary positions using a heliocentric model were easier to calculate, so some astronomers adopted this model as a "convenient fiction" (Principe 2011, 47–51).

Tycho Brahe (1546–1601)

Brahe spent more than thirty years collecting data on the planets' positions. He built his own position-measuring instruments and kept constantly improving them. Brahe's highly refined observations of stellar and planetary positions were much more accurate than those of any of his contemporaries. His improved data then provided the raw material for Kepler's efforts in looking for the overarching patterns that would describe the planets' movements in a compact and elegant manner (Ferguson 2002).

Johannes Kepler

Figure 3 Johannes Kepler

Kepler was a mystic, a meticulous worker, and a mathematician who fully accepted the Copernican results. He was a committed Christian humanist who consciously labored to show his work as an extension of the Greek classic works. Kepler spent many years laboriously going through Brahe's data, looking for simple compact mathematical patterns in it. Kepler first tried to fit circles to the data but, after many failures, realized that he needed to fit ellipses instead. He also discovered the equal area law, which states that a line drawn from the sun to a planet sweeps out equal areas in equal times as a planet moves (Ferguson 2002).

Galileo Galilei

Galileo's father was a distinguished musician. Galileo studied medicine at the University of Pisa. His preliminary courses in mathematics and natural philosophy encouraged him to devote himself to the study of numbers. He became a professor in mathematics at Pisa in 1589, where he taught for eighteen years.

Religious reaction to Copernicus before 1600 had been subdued largely because so few people thought his theory was correct. In 1610 Galileo published his *Sidereal Messenger* to publicize the discoveries he had made with a newly available piece of scientific equipment—the telescope. No one had ever seen or used a telescope for astronomy before! Galileo discovered that the moon was not a perfect sphere, as Aristotle had said all heavenly bodies must be, but was disfigured by craters and mountains. Also, Venus did not orbit Earth—it orbited the sun. When Galileo visited Rome in 1611, he received a hero's welcome, and the Jesuit astronomers lauded him openly for his wonderful discoveries.

Figure 4 Galileo Galilei

When Ptolemy's system was rendered obsolete by Galileo's discoveries, there were only two candidates to replace it—the ideas of Copernicus and those of Tycho Brahe.

In 1610, cashing in his newfound celebrity, Galileo took up the post of official mathematician to the grand Duke of Tuscany, Cosimo de Medici.

Back in the fourth century, Saint Augustine of Hippo had wrestled with the matter of what to do when the Bible and science said different things. In his commentary on the book of Genesis, he declared that when scripture and science differed, one should prefer to follow an allegorical interpretation of scripture. Carefully developing these early ideas of Saint Augustine, Galileo showed that in this particular case, the Bible should not be read as a scientific document, but one written in the language of the common people. Thus, when it referred to the sun "rising and setting," it was simply using the everyday idiom that everyone was familiar with.

Pope Urban VIII was an admirer of Galileo. They were both from Tuscany and had known each other for many years. Galileo was granted six audiences with the Pope during his stay in Rome, as well as a pension for Galileo's son. Urban VIII granted Galileo permission to publish his works as long as he presented his ideas as a hypothesis.

Before the dialogue could be printed, Galileo needed to obtain official sanction from the Congregation of the Index, which was an official institution that defined which books were not allowed to be published. After certain amount of negotiation, this was forthcoming, and the book came out in February 1632. Galileo called his defense of a heliocentric hypothesis *Dialogue Concerning the Two Chief World Systems: the Ptolemaic and the Copernican*. The three characters in the dialogue—Salviati (representing Galileo), Simplicio (a naive Aristotelian), and Sagredo (a not terribly neutral chairman)—engaged in discussion over four days. Simplicio's job was to put up the arguments that Galileo was to refute, which would invariably make Simplicio appear foolish. Galileo put the pope's argument about how God could engineer circumstances to produce any end result into the mouth of Simplicio. The pope's argument was weak and inimical to natural philosophy. By substituting it at the end, Galileo showed what he thought of it and thereby ensured that His Holiness would take umbrage. To make matters worse, this petty annoyance materialized while Urban VIII was overwhelmed by diplomatic negotiations regarding the ongoing Thirty Years' War, mounting criticism, attempts to depose him, and rumors of his impending death.

11

When the pope read Galileo's published document, he was furious! The pope ordered the book withdrawn and appointed a special commission to examine it. Galileo was summoned to Rome in February 1633 to stand trial for heresy. The problem for the Inquisition was that the Congregation of the Index had actually permitted the publication of the dialogue. How could they convict Galileo of heresy when he'd had their prior approval? Galileo's trial began on April 12, 1633. Galileo's sentence was commuted to house arrest, and Galileo returned home. Significantly, several cardinals including Urban's nephew refused to sign the sentence against Galileo. Folklore aside, Galileo was never condemned as a heretic, imprisoned, or chained. The pope ordered that copies of Galileo's sentence be dispatched throughout the Catholic world.

Galileo was sentenced to house arrest, and he began to write again and produced the book that sealed his reputation as a titan among mankind's intellectual champions. The new book, *Discourse on Two New Sciences*, had to be smuggled out and published by a printer in the Netherlands. Despite this, it was never banned by the Congregation of the Index. (Hannam 2000; Shea and Artiga 2003).

New Methods in Science

Methodologically, what Galileo ignored is as important as what he paid attention to. In describing motion, he never concerned himself with what was moving—a ball, an anvil, or a cow. In short, he ignored the qualities of bodies that Aristotelian physics emphasized. Galileo favored instead their quantities, their abstract mathematical properties. By stripping away an object's characteristics of shape, color, and composition, Galileo gave an idealized mathematical description of its behavior. A cold brown ball of oak doesn't fall any differently than a hot white cube of tin; Galileo reduced both objects to abstract, decontextualized entities able to be treated mathematically. Significantly, Galileo was content to describe motion mathematically without worrying about its cause. This feature of Galileo's work departed fundamentally from Aristotelian science, in which true knowledge is the knowledge of causes. Galileo's approach resembles that of an engineer—a person more interested in describing and utilizing what an object does than in trying to explain why it does it (Principe 2011, 72–3).

When Newton studied the forces of attraction between two bodies, he treated these bodies as point masses, ignoring their color, shape, and texture. It was this simplification that allowed him to develop his famous laws of force and motion. An object has primary qualities like mass, chemical composition, position, velocity, and acceleration. Secondary qualities are its color, shape, and emotional associations. In the spiritual domain, universal principles only take us so far; specifics such as our life history, our temperament, our surroundings, etc. can be of the essence! Don't abstract specifics away.

Figure 5 Isaac Newton

Isaac Newton (1643–1727)

Newton's laws of motion and gravity seemed applicable to all objects, from the smallest particle in the laboratory to the farthest planet. This was still a single harmonious order, as in the Middle Ages, but now it was a structure of forces and masses rather than a hierarchy of purposes. This magnificent synthesis of diverse domains was rightly admired, and the

13

perfection of mathematical law made a great impression on his contemporaries. It suggested an image of the world as an intricate machine following immutable laws, with every detail precisely predictable. Here was the basis for the philosophies of determinism and materialism that later generations were to develop...The properties that could be treated mathematically—mass and motion—were alone considered to be characteristics of the real world; other properties were taken to be purely subjective, having no existence outside the mind...In such a mechanical world, however, Newton himself still found room for both God and the human spirit (Barbour 1990, 18).

"Newton saw the task of natural philosophy as the restoration of the knowledge of the complete system of the cosmos, including God as the creator and as the ever-present Agent. Newton's law of universal gravitation obliterated the last traces of the former distinction between terrestrial and celestial Physics (Principe 2011, 65).

The universe was now visualized as being a mechanical clock built and wound up by God, after which every gear turned under complete control of the previous gear. The philosophies of materialism and determinism eventually resulted from this model.

Figure 6 Gears driving gears

Materialism: The doctrine that says that nothing exists except matter and its movements and modifications. If this is true, mind and free will do not exist.

The law of conservation of matter came from chemistry, in which it was a useful concept supported by experimental results in chemical reactions. Observing that matter seemed to be all pervasive and stable led to the idea that nothing but matter existed. Since then, we have learned that matter is not conserved, since matter can be turned into energy. We have also discovered that what we call matter accounts for a very small percentage of the universe, the oh-so-mysterious dark matter accounting for more than 90 percent. Materialism is a good example of the limitation of the method of induction, which starts with a finite sample of data and then makes universal predictions based on that.

Determinism: The belief that all events are caused and totally controlled by things that happened before them. The universe is here visualized as a mechanical clock set in motion by being wound up, after which every gear turns under complete control of the previous gear, following an unalterable path. If this is so, then human beings have no choice or free will.

Newton's work led to expressing descriptions of natural processes using linear differential equations. Knowing the differential equation and its initial conditions forced a unique response for the future behavior. From chaos theory, we now know that small errors in the initial conditions of some differential equations can lead to drastic changes in the equation's solutions.

The intelligence, broad range of interests, and dedication of Copernicus, Kepler, and Galileo have been a great inspiration to me. I'm proud to be a part of their endeavor! I am especially touched by realizing that my long-lived attraction to beauty proved to be such a part of their journey. It was also heartwarming to me to see that science can be guided and enriched by giving heed to the works of our great Western philosophers. No longer an orphan from classical

Greece, which I have always admired. I am in awe of the depth and breadth of these great thinkers!

Contrasting the Old and the New

Aristotle: True knowledge is the knowledge of causes.

Galileo: Describes motion numerically without attempting to explain why action at a distance exists.

Aristotle: Qualities such as color, shape, and texture are important.

Galileo: Treat an object as a point mass. Simplify, leave out details, only quantities are important.

Aristotle: Abstract thinking is predominant.

Galileo: Include hands-on experiments, use instruments, then process results logically.

Aristotle: *Why* does the object do what it does? (Seek purpose, meaning "Why?") Seeks to explain.

Galileo: *What* does the object *do*? (Just describe "How?") Seeks to describe.

Aristotle: Appeal to universal principles. Use deduction from first principles.

Galileo: Take experimental results and then generalize them. Go from specific to universal.

"First, you know, a new theory is attacked as absurd; then it is admitted to be true, but obvious and insignificant; finally, it is seen to be so important that its adversaries claim that they themselves discovered it" (James 1907, 87).

16

The Experimental Method

Galileo made experimentation an essential requisite for acquiring knowledge about the physical world. Broadly speaking, his method requires advance planning and setup of equipment, change of one variable at a time, measuring and interpreting of data, ending in generalizing the results through the use of induction. Many disciplines have attempted to emulate Galileo's approach. These diverse specialties, which today run into the thousands, may have had to make adaptations to their methods of performing experiments appropriate to their fields, giving to the word *science* a wide variety of meanings. I will use this word throughout this book as originally intended by Galileo.

Summary

The Galileo affair was not a science-versus-religion conflict; rather, it involved at least four important elements:
- The large-scale conflicts of the Reformation made the institutional church overreact.
- The threat to Aristotelian philosophy, which pervaded scholarly thought at that time.
- Galileo had made many enemies because of his combative personality.
- Pope Urban VIII's sense of betrayal and public humiliation (Tarnas 1991, 260).

Afterthoughts

The deep religious and devotional incentive that motivated early modern natural philosophers to study the Book of Nature—to find the Creator reflected in the creation—no longer provides a major driving force for scientific research.

The constant awareness of history, of being part of a long and cumulative tradition of inquirers into nature, has been largely lost. Few scientists today would do as Kepler did when he subtitled his Copernican textbook, *A Supplement to Aristotle*, or seek for answers in ancient texts where Newton sought for gravity's cause.

The vision of a tightly interconnected cosmos has been fractured by the abandonment of questions of meaning and purpose, by narrowed perspectives and aims, and by a preference for a literalism ill-equipped to comprehend the analogy and metaphor fundamental to early modern thought.

The natural philosopher in his broad scope of thought, activity, experience, and expertise has been supplanted by the professionalized, specialized, and technical scientist. The result is a scientific domain disconnected from the broader vistas of human culture and existence.

It is impossible not to think ourselves the poorer for the loss of a comprehensive early modern vision, even while we are bound to acknowledge that modern scientific and technological development has enriched us with an astonishing level of material and intellectual wealth (Principe 2011, 134 ff.).

> The fatal metaphor of progress, which means leaving things behind us, has utterly obscured

the real idea of growth, which means leaving things inside us.

—G. K. Chesterton

Modern science originally covered a bounded and focused field of study (physics and fields derived from it). As science dazzled the world with its many successes, it started to expand into other fields. By the 1800s, it eventually started being treated as the only way to find truth in all fields of study. Disciplines that did not claim to be scientific could lose their credibility. Even philosophy was under pressure to become scientific. Since the 1900s we hopefully are moving towards a new-found humility when learning of the limitations of our knowing the physical universe.

Personal Reflections

After I researched the Galileo affair, three things stood out for me: the curiosity, sense of wonder, intelligence and dedication that was shown; the deep bond between spirituality and science present in all work; and the conscious inclusion of philosophy with science. The technical core of the Galileo affair cannot be understood without going back to Pythagoras and Plato!

I resent seeing our present-day tear among these three awesome worlds of philosophy, spirituality, and science. For myself, I resolve to go beyond petty differences, personalities, and historical setting and keep my former awareness of philosophy, religion, and science all consciously active and cherished by me.

For Further Reading

Barbour, Ian G. 1990. *Religion and Science: Historical and Contemporary Issues*, San Francisco: Harper One.

A classic in the field of the constructive dialog between science and religion.

Kuhn, Thomas S. 1985. *The Copernican Revolution: Planetary Astronomy in the Development of Western Thought*. Cambridge, MA: Harvard University Press.
A scholarly overview of the significance of Copernicus' achievements in the history and philosophy of science.

Finochiaro, Maurice A., ed. and trans. 2008. *The Essential Galileo*. Indianapolis, IN: Hackett Publishing Company,
All essential reference documents written by Galileo are expertly translated into English and are made available in one book.

Shea, William R., and Mariano Artiga. 2003. *Galileo in Rome: The Rise and Fall of a Troublesome Genius*. New York: Oxford University Press.
A detailed account of the time Galileo spent in Rome. Written from archival documents by two scholars.

Ferguson, Kitty. 2008. *The Music of Pythagoras*. New York: Walker and Company.
A skillful and thorough tracing of the impact of the thought of Pythagoras on Western science throughout the centuries until today.

Sheldrake, Rupert. 2012. *Science Set Free: 10 Paths to New Discovery*. New York: Deepak Chopra Books.

Cvitenovic, Predrag. 1989. *Universality in Chaos*, 2nd ed. New York: Taylor and Francis Group, LLC.

Freely, John. 2012. *Before Galileo: The Birth of Modern Science in Medieval Europe*. New York: Overlook Duckworth, Peter Mayer Publishers.

Chapter 2
Important Differences in Language

Many years ago, I was sitting in a small-town barbershop awaiting my turn. The customer getting his hair cut had lived in that small town all his life. He had just returned from his first vacation ever taken outside the country. The barber asked him for his impressions of his trip. The customer got very agitated. He exclaimed, "It was terrible! These people, they didn't even speak English! Can you believe this? I'm never going back again!"

Have you ever found yourself in a foreign country trying to communicate in the local language and experienced great frustration? Have you ever tried to help out a foreign tourist who is lost in your city? We take language for granted until we are in a situation in which our native tongue loses its power to communicate, leaving us feeling frustrated and helpless.

There is a sharp dividing line between the essential working languages of science and spirituality. It can be very helpful for someone trained in the physical sciences who is trying to deepen his or her spiritual life to first become sensitized to how the language of spirituality can be different in some ways from the language of science.

Cultures

When we cross borders from one culture to another, some problems can arise immediately; one of these is the problem of ethnocentrism.

- Ethnocentricity: "The view in which one's own group is the center of everything, and all others are scaled and rated with reference to it." Feelings that "we are right and they are wrong" (Samovar and Porter 2000, 10).

We are all born, raised, and educated within the domain of one specific culture. To actively participate in another culture requires effort and openness from us. The cardinal rule for entering another culture is to stay open to acknowledging the value of its distinctive characteristics, even if they seem peculiar to us. Viewing this culture through its own frame of reference can allow us to take in what is really happening there. We need to slowly immerse ourselves as much as possible in their mind-sets, circumstances, and language. We need to suspend judgment before we can see things from their vantage point. This is hard to do; we must allow ourselves to go through a period of confusion and disorientation before we begin to understand our new surroundings.

To enter the world of physical science, one must accept the experimental techniques of scientific work plus its associated language of mathematics. To enter the world of spirituality, one needs to respond to the languages of literature and art.

I will now present a short review of some important issues in the differences between the languages of science and spirituality. Let's review some properties of written human language first. We will discuss spoken language in a later chapter.

The Need for Different Languages

I have a vivid memory of an experience I had one day while working at a semiconductor company. In the morning, we discovered that the software we had written did not always work—it had a bug! I spent the morning deeply immersed in flowcharts and computer language. In the afternoon, I wrestled with problems having to do with a laboratory experiment involving semiconductor material properties responding to temperature and voltage levels. That same evening at home, I struggled with my role as a husband

and father with my family. Without being aware of it, I had been forced to use three specialized languages that same day: the rigid, abstract, manmade language of programming in the morning; the language of the experimental method in the afternoon; and that evening, the human language of feelings, affection, bonding, and relatedness with my family. The three languages I used that day were separately fine-tuned to their application and were not interchangeable. I cannot use software language to solve family relatedness problems. I can't use semiconductor equations to solve a software bug.

- All science workers are commuters, daily shuttling between cultures that utilize languages different from one another.

A language used in a field of knowledge reflects the focused range of interest and priorities in that field. Every discipline has its own objects under study, their properties, and the appropriate language used to describe and work with them. From a broad point of view, we can say that each one of the branches of physical science utilizes the language of mathematics, plus a specialized technical language that is appropriate to that particular branch.

In my personal life, I was inevitably confronted with these essential human issues: How do I cope with suffering? What is the meaning of life? Is there a God? What is worthy of my love, and how do I grow in that direction? What things should I value the most? What constitutes good or evil behavior? What is beauty, and why does it exist? How should I relate to the universe? Facing these essential issues that arise from the core of being a human being, I found out that my previous knowledge of the languages of math, physics, and biology was not enough. I discovered that I needed a language quite different from the technical languages I had used. I needed a language that could process meaning, value, love, suffering, emotions. This language is the language of spirituality and has been around for as long as humanity has been struggling on this Earth. Many parts of this language look surprisingly like the languages of literature, poetry, and the arts in general.

When we research new findings in science, trying to understand them better by forming helpful concepts, we find that these concepts will invariably be expressed in the form of mathematical models: equations, data tables, word statements, graphs, or software. In trying to understand the concepts of spirituality or reflecting on what we find in our inner world, we find that we need to use metaphors, story, and symbols. Language is a conceptual tool. The conceptual tool being used at any time must fit its present application: mathematical models for science, literature for spiritual concepts and our inner world. This split in languages has been one factor in the formation and reinforcement of two separate cultures over the years, one for science and one for spirituality.

Speed Reading

During my lengthy studies in college, I became painfully aware that I could never do the vast amount of reading required by my courses unless I drastically changed my reading habits. I learned to survive by quickly becoming adept at speed reading. I learned how to scan a whole page very quickly, only looking for key items, then instantly moving on to the next page. Even later, when doing research in industry, I could take in the contents of thick instrument manuals or system specifications by only performing quick scans. The habit of speed reading became so ingrained in me that I found I now had trouble reading novels or poetry when at home.

Reading spiritual works is the exact opposite of speed reading! Slow is better. Less is better. We need to read very slowly, allowing time for the text to touch us, to evoke inner responses. Spiritual writings are commonly meant to elicit a response from us, sometimes touching us at a deep level. There is a wise saying: "Music does not consist of notes, but the spaces between them," which means that the effect of music consists of our response to the sounds, not the sounds themselves.

- Spiritual writings take effect in us during our interior response time, the spaces between the words.

Denotations

A word has two properties: denotation, and connotation. Denotation consists of the dictionary meaning(s) attached to a word (Perrine and Arp 1993).

The five hundred words most commonly used in everyday language have an average of half a dozen meanings each. Human language contains a strong element of ambiguity! No wonder we have so many misunderstandings, breakups, and wars! As an example, here are listed the dictionary meanings (denotations) of the word *term* taken from *Webster's Dictionary*:

Term: 1. End, termination; 2. Limited or definite extent of time; 3. A fixed period of time, as when a court is in session; 4. Division in a school year; 5. Part of a mathematical expression separated from others by a plus or minus sign; 6. One of the three substantive elements of a syllogism; 7. Word or expression which has precise meaning in some uses; 8. Provisions for an agreement; 9. Mutual relationship; 10. Boundary post (Webster's Seventh New Collegiate Dictionary 1967).

To resolve the ambiguity of this word's denotations requires looking into the context of the situation involved and may also require asking questions for clarification.

"The purest form of practical language is scientific language (math). Scientists need a precise language to convey information precisely...Their ideal language would be a language with a one-to-one correspondence between word and meaning...stripped of all denotations but one" (Perrine and Arp 1993, 557).

Connotations

There is a second important meaning of a word: its connotation. This is very important because it includes the individual emotional response of the reader. "The connotations of a word consist of what the word suggests beyond what it expresses: its overtones of meaning. It acquires these connotations by its past history and associations, by the way and the circumstances in which it has been used" (Perrine and Arp 1993, 557).

Note that connotations can have powerful emotional content, but this content can also have a great deal of ambiguity to it. The word *home* may suggest comfort to one person and loss to another while eliciting painful memories of conflict from yet a third person.

An analogy for connotations: playing middle *C* on a variety of musical instruments creates similar yet different sounds because each instrument generates a unique set of harmonics. These harmonics give each instrument its unique "voice."

When someone is trying to share something personally difficult or embarrassing with us, he or she will skirt around the issue. Our role as a loving friend is then to discern the emotional connotations of what he or she dares not speak out loud.

- The presence and energy of the connotation of a word implies that "intended message sent" may be quite different from "message received."

My experience in working in technical denotation-only environments has been that this literal mode of communicating, unfortunately, can inadvertently carry over into our human relations as well. In a highly technical setting, business communication must be very short, simple, and to the point, emphasizing denotation exclusively (fact-and-run communication). On the other hand, person-to-person relationships require us to switch gears and stay alert for the connotation and the personal associations that go with people's speech. If we listen to denotation only, we are at risk of dehumanizing our relationships with others. It takes some effort to switch from denotation-only to compassionate listening. We desperately need to do this, always staying tuned to what connotations the other person may be experiencing as we talk!

For example, if a work acquaintance approaches me and says "One of my parents has taken seriously ill," the meaning (literal denotation) is very clear. I need to go beyond the denotation and, using my imagination and compassion, fill in the picture of the devastating effect this event will have on the whole family. My support and caring are being called for here.

The Working Language of Science

The essential working language of physical science commonly uses some four or five modes to communicate the same information in different formats: the data table, the graph, the equation, and the word statement. Because of the pervasive use of computers, we may also add software to the above forms. Besides words from mathematics, special-purpose jargon terms with single

28

denotations such as *entropy*, *magnetic*, *field*, *velocity*, and so on may also be used.

We have access to five possible ways of describing the results of an experiment.

- **Data table:** Numerical data is collected from the instruments used in the experiment and is then written in an orderly table form.
- **Graph:** Representing the contents of the data table in the form of a graph lends itself to providing visual insights into data patterns.
- **Equation:** If the data collected is similar to a known math function, this data can be curve-fitted to that function, thus allowing the convenient use of math operations on the data.
- **Software model:** A mathematical software model is created to be used in a software simulation program, which allows solving problems that require large amounts of difficult computation.
- **Word description:** The lab setup, instrumentation problems encountered, interpretation of the results, future work needed, and so on can be described here.

The essential working language of science includes math signs such as $+$ (plus), $-$ (minus), $=$ (equals), X (variable), and X^2 (squared).

The essential working language of science is meant to be completely unambiguous, compact, and minimalist, intentionally leaving out any extraneous information. It is meant to produce a one-to-one relationship between what is being said and what is being read. In other words, there is a single denotation. The language of science is impersonal; it is independent of the author and of the recipient. It is unemotional and detached.

On the negative side, the language of science is exclusivist, since it requires specialized user training and practice in order to understand and use it. The purpose of this language is to communicate numerical data and its patterns in an unambiguous way and with clarity, which can lead to technical insight.

Note: The fact that math has a high degree of precision does not automatically mean that our models are just as accurate in describing reality. My experience spending many years in the laboratory taking measurements has taught me to view mathematical models as only approximate, tentative guides to represent reality. We must not confuse the model with the process it attempts to represent!

> Mathematics is the door and the key to the sciences.
> —Francis Bacon

> If you can measure that of which you speak, and can express it by a number, you know something of your subject; but if you cannot measure it, your knowledge is meager and unsatisfactory.
> —William Thomas, Lord Kelvin
> British Physicist (1824–1907)

The very nature of the mathematical language of science means that it can be used to represent only things that can be described by a number that can be measured or calculated. In the physical sciences, this would be obviously only objects and processes containing length, mass, time, force, charge, and so on. The International System of Units (SI) gives us the worldwide standards for units used for measuring the basic physical quantities.

Only things whose important properties can be reduced to jargon and numbers can be handled by math and science. Try

30

quantifying love, fear, joy, beauty, justice, envy, anxiety, death, meaning, value, morality. You will find that these essential human issues cannot be meaningfully quantified. Since these issues are an inescapable part of human life, we need access to a language other than math to grapple with these issues.

Exercise

Attempt to express the following experiences using an equation (involving mass, distance, force, temperature, electrical charge...) that would communicate this experience objectively to a stranger:

- Your first kiss
- Being present at the death of a loved one
- Impressions on your first visit to the Grand Canyon
- Your response to viewing a Rembrandt self-portrait
- Experiencing rejection
- Listening to your favorite song
- A hurtful memory

Math Signs Contrasted with Literary Symbols

The essential language of mathematics is special purpose. It is meant to clearly communicate one and only one meaning, a unique denotation using numbers and math signs. I will very intentionally use the word *sign* to refer to the elements that are used in algebraic notation such as *add, subtract, multiply, exponent, equals, variable*, and so on.

- A sign in mathematics has a single predefined meaning that represents either a number or an operation on numbers.

- "In contrast to a sign, a [literary] symbol can be an object, a person, a situation, an action, or some other item that has a literal meaning in a story but suggests or represents other meanings as well…The [literary] symbol is the richest, and at the same time, most difficult of the poetic figures. Both its richness and its difficulty arise from its imprecision" (Perrine and Arp 1993, 194 and 600).

A literary symbol can have a wide range of meanings. Here are some examples of symbols:

- Objects: a wedding ring, a flowering weed growing out of a crack in the sidewalk, Mount Everest, a casket, the flag, a run-down house, Ellis Island, a candle flickering in the dark.

- Persons: Hitler, Martin Luther King, a sleeping baby, a homeless person.

- Situations: daybreak, twilight, immigrant arrivals, a wedding ceremony, a drought, the first snowfall, the dark at the top of the stairs, the cry of a newborn baby.

- Actions: embracing, turning over the car keys to my sixteen-year-old son or daughter for the first time, a plane taxiing on the runway, turning one's back on someone, a twenty-one-gun salute, sharing a home-cooked meal together.

- Math sign: Has a single predetermined denotation or meaning. Its one meaning is independent of both the writer and the reader.

- Literary symbol: Means what it is and something more. Its multiple meanings depend on the writer, the context or setting, the reader, and his or her personal associations.

In religion, the word *symbol* has a specialized meaning that is much richer and more complex than its use in science. In order to provide more clarity to this discussion, I will use the word *sign* only to indicate the elements of algebraic notation and *symbol* to describe a literary symbol.

A literary symbol points to something other than itself. A literary symbol also participates in that to which it points. A literary symbol has the power to evoke responses from us. These responses are multiple and vary from person to person and even within the same person in different contexts and at different times. For example, I will experience different responses to the American flag at different ages. When I behold the flag as a child, I am thrilled by its waving and shininess. As a teenager, I might think of what I learned in school about history. As a new army recruit, I can feel a new sense of identifying with the flag. When I am a battle veteran attending a military burial ceremony, I may be left speechless, aware of the force of human evil, and full of grief.

Working with Literary Symbols

To understand the meanings of any given literary symbol, it is necessary to spend some time reflecting upon it; it requires some postprocessing effort. Since literary symbols are highly compressed expressions, they can speak to us with a single word or phrase use our imaginations and creativity to expand a literary symbol's meanings as it speaks to us. This process is called symbol amplification. Here is an example of amplification of literary symbols:

When I Heard the Learn'd Astronomer

> When I heard the learn'd astronomer,
> When the proofs, the figures, were arranged
> in columns before me,
> When I was shown the charts and diagrams,
> to add, divide,
> and measure them,
> When I sitting heard the astronomer where he
> lectured with much applause in the lecture—
> room,
> How soon unaccountable I became tired and
> sick,
> Till rising and gliding out I wander'd off by
> myself,
> In the mystical moist night air, and from time
> to time,
> Look'd up in perfect silence at the stars.
>
> —Walt Whitman
> Leaves of Grass

Here are some of my personal subjective responses to the literary symbols in this poem. You may have some other associations of your own. Let's see what your own responses might be.

- *Charts and diagrams*: The awe-inspiring experience of contemplating the nighttime sky is being reduced to numbers only. The infinite is being reduced to the finite and mundane.
- *I sitting heard*: Accepting the presentation passively.

- He lectured with much applause: Group think.
- *Unaccountable I became sick and tired*: I am aware of something being very wrong, but I can't put it into words, yet I feel a revulsion inside me.
- *Rising*: I take steps to break away from the collective mind-set.
- *Mystical moist night air*: I experience a living presence that is personal, invigorating, refreshing, freeing.
- *The stars*: The cosmos, God.
- *Looked up*: Seeking a higher ground, rising above the mundane everyday level.
- *In perfect silence*: My experience is ineffable, beyond words. (American philosopher and psychologist William James did a study of mystical experiences, and one quality they all had in common was that they could not be verbalized; they were beyond words.)

Here's another example of the use of symbols to communicate an abstract concept: "The wind blows where it chooses, and you hear the sound of it, but you do not know where it comes from or where it is going. So it is with everyone who is born of the Spirit" (John 3:8).

Notice what a powerful symbol wind is! We are surrounded by air, yet we're not aware of its presence. We can't see it. We can't normally hear it. Reflection tells us that everything around us that's alive—plants, animals and ourselves—depends on that invisible stuff to keep us alive. At certain times that invisible energy can change on us unpredictably. It can change direction; it can become intense; it can break down houses. It can bring down rain.

The literary symbol of wind is one of invisibility, all-pervasiveness, powerful and life-giving, yet capable of destroying all. The presence or absence of air makes the difference between life and death for all of us.

Here is another example of symbol amplification. Picture that you are sitting in a dark chapel in which a single candle is burning in the dark.

Here is a list of my personal responses and associations:

- It attracts me, yet I can't touch it since it can burn me.
- It dispels only a limited amount of darkness.
- It pushes the darkness (death) away, but only temporarily.
- I can see only because of it.
- It gives light by consuming itself (self-giving).
- Fragile, yet also strong.
- Constantly moving, changing, transient.
- Warm, yet surrounded by cold (like my living body).
- Breathes air, the same as I.
- Almost seems to have life, a soul.
- Gives off a faint smell (presence).

The Three Regions of Knowing

Figure 7 Three regions of knowing

1. **What is known** (center circle): Your address, weight, age, Social Security number, school degrees.

2. **What is not known but can be known** (middle region): Your great-grandparents' names, your full DNA sequence, the results of your technical work, the survival of our planet.

3. **Mystery** (outer area): The full extent of the universe, why humans are the way we are, why gravity exists, what electrical charge is.

I had difficulty accepting mystery into my life, but if I hadn't, I never would have said yes to love and family life.

Metaphor

I was walking in a park one day. A father was walking his three-year-old in front of me. Suddenly, a small cat darted across the path and disappeared into the bushes. The little boy was ecstatic; his whole body shook from excitement as he blurted out, "Doggy!" The dad responded by correcting him and telling him that was a kitty, not a doggy. I reflected on this, and I realized that the little boy had done something very natural. He had identified the unknown by equating it to the known (a small nonhuman creature with four legs and fur). This illustrates one natural way we all generate metaphors.

When doing technical work, we deal with things such as pressure, voltage, pH, and so on. All these physical parameters can be measured or calculated numerically.

An example: if a voltage V1 in an electronic circuit is unknown to me, I can measure it with a voltmeter or calculate it using software and then know its value. We would then say:

$$V1 = 2.75 \text{ Volts}$$
(unknown) is equal to (known)

The essential connection between the unknown and the known is the equal sign.

We normally can't use an equal sign to connect two numbers in the field of spirituality. The things that concern spirituality, such as meditation, insight, personal growth, love, suffering, compassion, and attentiveness cannot be measured numerically.

- Quite often, spirituality deals with things that we can experience and know at a deep level, yet are very difficult or perhaps even impossible to verbalize or define.

Try to define fear, love, compassion, or meaning in such a way that someone else would know exactly what you meant! For these two reasons, we need something other than the equals sign (=) in spiritual writings.

- The counterpart of = in science in spiritual writing is a metaphor.

  "The Lord *is* my shepherd."
  (unknown) is like (known)

A metaphor is a comparison of two things. It compares an unknown to a tangible, familiar known. We use (or imply) the words *is* or *are*, to indicate not an equality but an important similarity.

Creating a new metaphor usually comes to us as a flash of insight, an *Aha!* or a *Eureka!*, seeing an important commonality that connects/compares an unknown to something tangible and familiar. The use of metaphors is so pervasive throughout our lifetime that if we use a metaphor repeatedly, it is easy to unconsciously think it is literally true. It comes as a surprise when we realize that an expression we have been using for a long time is figuratively, not literally, true!

In the field of science, we use software to solve problems that, because of their size or complexity, can't be conveniently solved by simple reasoning or by hand calculations. We are often faced with a problem such as a complicated equation that we need to solve. We write software that will act as a metaphor for our given problem and then proceed to let the computer solve the metaphor numerically. Occasionally, we are surprised when the simulator gives us a wrong answer, reminding us of the following:

- A computer-simulated model is not identical to, but a metaphor for, our real-life technical problem.

Some Examples of Metaphors

(See the back of the book for a more extensive list.)

Scientists are *unlocking* the secrets of the universe.
Data *bus*, input *port*, *mother*board, *cloud* computing
Software *platform*, file *folder*, software *bug*
Enter the kingdom of Heaven.
He is *moving up* in the company.
Suddenly, a *light* went on in my mind.
Eyes are the *windows* of the soul.
He is *going through* a period of *dryness*.
He has a *closed* mind.
New vistas *opened up* for me with my promotion.
I *moved up* to a *higher plane*.
I'm feeling *up* today.
I was *down* all winter.
That artist had a rich *inner* world; the *outer* world did not concern him as much.
He *rose* to fame; I *fell down* on my diet.
The *core* of our being, the *center* of all our motivation
Right side (stronger, more control), *left side* (weaker, less control).
As I struggled with a problem, suddenly, *a light went on.*
Light, sun, candle: insight, awareness, understanding
Darkness: confusion, ignorance, mistrust
Save, redeem: turn around for the better, healing change, enlighten.

Literalism

Literalism involves identifying a statement exclusively with its denotation; confusing a metaphor with an identity; or in science, confusing a model with the thing it models.

Literalism is appropriate at times, but at other times, it can lead to rigidity, shortsightedness, and defensiveness in thinking. Literalism can occur not only in religion, but in science as well. The obvious question arises: How do I know when to take a metaphor or a physical model literally and when figuratively? The answer is a real-life answer: while staying open, use your judgment, consult with others whose opinion you value. If you can't resolve this question, accept that you need to learn to live with uncertainty for now. Uncertainty and ambiguity are facts of Quantum Mechanics and of life!

Within science, when we can take a model to be totally true without any restrictions, we can close our mind to seeing that the model is only an approximation, and it may at times need refining, reinterpreting, or replacing. We need to stay open to situations in which the model fails us and we need to reevaluate it. Many breakthroughs in science take place when an accepted model does not produce results that match our data, forcing us to reconsider our thinking. We see this happening very clearly when Copernicus overthrew the Ptolemaic planetary model.

Consider some of the early models for the atom. Each one was a model, or metaphor, useful as a tool to explain the observed measurements:

- Plum pudding model of J. J Thomson (1904). The atom is made up of discrete electrons surrounded by a "soup" of positive charge, just like raisins in a plum pudding.
- Ernest Rutherford model (1911): A great deal of mass and charge concentrated in the center, surrounded by a cloud of orbiting electrons.

41

- Bohr planetary model (1913): A dense central region surrounded by electrons, which orbit the nucleus like planets in discrete orbits.

In using metaphors, we should remember that a metaphor contains a useful element of truth, yet at the same time might also contain an element of partial truth or nontruth. Keeping this in mind, we should be careful with literalism, which takes metaphors as being literally true.

Common tools used to allow us to move forward by equating the unknown back to the known:

- In science, we use the model.
- In spirituality, we use the metaphor.

Story

I have fond memories of many years spent reading bedtime stories to my two boys, never realizing that stories played a very special part in the lives of grown-ups across the ages. When I hear the word *story*, I sometimes experience an immediate knee-jerk negative reaction: "This is for children only, for short-lived entertainment only! Not worthy of my attention, a fabrication or, worse yet, a lie!" or "That was some story he made up to cover himself!"

Cultural anthropologists tell us that all known human cultures worldwide have used storytelling to communicate the deep truths of their cultures and religious worldviews. Archaeologists have found written records of stories dating as far back as four thousand years ago (Haviland 1987). Even prior to the invention of writing, stories were transmitted from generation to generation by word of mouth for as long as religions have been practiced worldwide. Quite an impressive track record!

In the absence of writing, preliterate cultures used stories as memory or mnemonic devices. It is much easier to recall and be touched by a story than it is to memorize abstract teachings. Abstract teachings have many separate abstract words associated with them, whereas a story uses concrete words and actions with unifying themes that hold all its parts together. Here is an example of an abstract teaching: philosopher Baruch Spinoza's definition of the concept of substance: "By substance I understand what is and is conceived through itself, i.e., that whose concept does not require the concept of another thing, from which it must be formed" (Spinoza 1985).

You can see the difficulties in being able to understand or remember this statement! This is one reason teaching stories can be so important as mnemonic devices.

I would conclude from all the above that storytelling is a deeply meaningful, integral part of what it means to be human, and I'd better pay attention, putting aside the preconceptions my technical schooling may have given me. I will not be listening to stories as a child but as an adult, aware of levels of meaning other than the literal, such as the uses of metaphor and symbol.

- So, what is a teaching story? Story is a narrative that illustrates significant choices and actions of characters over time. The character in the story is a bundle of values whose choices and actions reveal his or her attitudes and values. Story is an action narrative that may be historical in full detail, a modification of an historic event, or totally independent of history, created solely for the purpose of engaging/teaching the listener (Taylor 1995).

A story does not exclusively describe external events; it is useful in describing our experiences in the inner world: experiences during prayer, meditations, received insights, moments of illumination, and so on. The actors, the settings, and the actions in a story can take on universal symbolic values, which are true of all cultures and time periods worldwide. All the most ancient wisdom traditions worldwide have used sacred stories to communicate their deepest insights into the big picture of life.

Life is a never-ending succession of transitions and growing-up experiences. We learn some things in life through studying; some through following examples of others; and some through our own personal experiences, what we call "the school of hard knocks." A teaching story passes on to us an experience that we can live vicariously, learn from, and grow from, without actually having to undergo the hard knocks.

We find an analogy to the use of teaching stories in our time in the use of software flight simulators for the training of future airplane pilots. The flight simulator allows trainees to go through a variety of challenging experiences without ever actually crashing an expensive plane or endangering their own lives or the lives of others. We can think of spiritual teaching stories as deep-level "life simulators" that draw us into themselves to immerse us in their wisdom of accumulated experience, so we can then live rich, meaningful lives without hurting ourselves or others.

Here is another way to look at the function of story. Let's make an analogy. When we take a set of data measurements in the lab, we get a bunch of numbers. We then "connect the dots" to see the shape of the curve. When we are able to replace this set of numbers with an equation, we get an *Aha!* from being able to perceive the pattern behind the points. Story can compactly express the pattern that lies behind the scattered data of universal life experiences.

A Rough Analogy

Story can be to *life experiences*
as
equation is to *data points*.

Put these ideas to the test: visualize yourself explaining to a new friend you have just met your beliefs and deeply held values and how you came by them; you will invariably find that you are telling a story! A shallow friendship is like a job application: nothing but an impersonal chronological listing of generic facts. A deep friendship, on the other hand, includes the sharing of life stories, knowledge of our past, our struggles, successes, failures, feelings, and values. We experience our lives as one long, rambling story with many twists and turns to it, all personal, subjective, and concrete.

- Story is not only for children, but for all.
- Story adds to our experience bank.
- Story moves us and teaches us.
- Story can produce powerful permanent changes in us.

A great achievement of the twentieth century was the discovery of the human subconscious/unconscious. To be fully awake as human beings, we need to be conversant with our unconscious. The essential language of the human unconscious has been shown to consist of symbol and story (Jung et al. 1964). Symbol and story are deep, essential parts of our humanity today, the same as they have been for thousands of years!

Suggestions for Listening to a Story

1. Temporarily suspend disbelief, become receptive, childlike.

2. Using your imagination, immerse yourself in the setting of the narrative. If foreign settings or names give you trouble, feel free to modify them to something more familiar to you.

3. Feel the emotions of the participants in the story and identify with them. Actively participate in the action.

4. Look for symbols, themes, and values being expressed, and meditate on them, so you can expand these symbols based on your personal life experience.

5. Identify the important values and character traits of the actors.

6. Write a brief summary of your response to the story.

Example: Psalm 5:3

For at daybreak you listen for my voice and
at dawn I hold myself in readiness for you.
—Psalms 5:3

I will now interpret this part of a psalm not as a literal narrative, but as a short teaching story meant to describe a long-term life experience that is common to many and, as such, has universal value.

At daybreak: I am not quite awake or conscious, at the threshold of alertness, before I even can have self-awareness.

You listen: God is caring, attentive, reaching out, taking initiative, anticipating my unspoken needs.

For my voice: recognizing my uniqueness, my identity, a call to relationship.

And at dawn: I am barely becoming aware of things.

I hold myself in readiness: I accept my limitedness; I admit neediness.

For you: my dependence is on God.

God even anticipates my being able to express my needs! God treats me as unique, special, in a one-on-one relationship when I am needy and losing control.

As I reflect over my past life, I am aware of times when I was needy yet did not have full awareness of what I really needed. Many years later, in retrospect, I can see what my need was at that time and how God answered my call.

Theme

- "Theme is the central and unifying concept of a story. The story needs to go beyond simply stating a point, it needs to vivify this point by appealing to the senses, emotions, and imagination of the reader" (Perrine and Arp 1993, 92).

Notice that the theme does not appear explicitly in the narrative. Note that in contrast to scientific language, which is meant to be independent of the reader, story has the involvement of the reader as one of its main objectives.

As we internalize the theme of a story, our reservoir of lived life experience increases. We grow by vicarious experience through identifying with the persons in the story. Theme communicates with the deepest unconscious levels of our minds.

Here is an example of finding symbols and themes in a story. Let's look at *Toy Story 3* (Walt Disney Pixar Animation Studios). The story opens with teenager Andy preparing to leave home to go to college. His bedroom is full of toys he's had all throughout his childhood. His mom has asked him to empty out his bedroom and put all his toys away into three boxes marked Attic, Donate, and Garbage.

Attic can symbolize an acknowledgment of the value these toys have had in his life and his realization that an attachment still remains. He just can't get rid of them for now.

Garbage can symbolize discarding that which is no longer of use. Andy has moved on and matured. An important life transition has occurred.

Donate can symbolize the ability to painfully let go of attachments while still having an empathetic awareness of others and their needs.

Woody, a toy cowboy, has been Andy's favorite toy since his childhood. There is a deep bond between the two of them.

Andy takes the box full of toys, including Woody, and gives it to a neighbor, a little four-year-old girl named Bonnie.

Here are some of the themes I see in this story: impermanence, moving into the unknown, bonding, group loyalty, returning love for love received, the painful awareness of the passing away of a life stage while letting go and responding to this loss by transcending self-absorption, not with anger or withdrawal or self-destructive behavior, but reaching out with love and empathy for others.

Comparison of Written Languages

Science: uses numerical quantities and technical terms.

Spirituality: uses metaphor, theme, symbol, and story, plus all the tools of literature, poetry, and drama.

Science: seeks to know or control physical processes that are external to us. Precision is important.

Story: seeks to promote our inner growth and self-awareness by enlarging our life-experience base. Its insightful and evocative qualities are important.

Some Limitations of the Language of Science

It can only describe physical processes, leaving out our inner lives. Formal training in math, plus specialized equipment and facilities are needed.

Some Limitations of the Language of Spirituality

Multiple interpretations can result because of the built-in ambiguity of the language used. "Message received" will be influenced by the receiver's culture, past history, stage in life, and openness.

Some Strengths of Scientific Language

It has one and only one denotation; its technical meaning is independent of sender or receiver.

Its measurements can be compared to standards.

Some Strengths of the Language of Spirituality

It is natural to all humanity across the miles and ages.

It can change our lives by touching us at depth.

Inner Silence

There is a large, deep expanse within us in which human language does not exist. This is hard to accept! We are so used to putting our thoughts into words that we forget the silence that preceded the words.

Creative insights, both in science and in spirituality, take place in silence. I have noticed that when struggling to solve a technical problem, the solution slowly begins to materialize before I can even express it in words. Sometimes verbalizing our new insight can be just as hard as arriving at it! How often we say "I can't put it into words!" or "The solution just came to me!"

> A mind enclosed in language is in prison.
> —Simone Weil
> Activist, philosopher, and mystic

> True creativity often starts where language ends.
> —Arthur Koestler
> Writer

Our training in science has taught us to observe external reality and then express our response by words and math signs. All the action appears to be taking place externally to us and can be described by spoken words. Obviously, science cannot exist without the use of language. What may not be so obvious is that science also depends on our creative insights, which come to us during periods of silence!

Have you ever found yourself speechless? I certainly have! Here are three experiences that filled me with awe and taught me the value, the truthfulness, the depths, the inevitability of silence:

- Falling in love
- The birth of my two sons
- Being present at the death of my firstborn son

Think about your early childhood years of development, when innumerable, deep, essential changes took place in your body and mind prior to your even knowing how to speak. These experiences, as processed by a child, are still important parts of your world view even though you can't verbalize them today.

Reflecting on your peak life experiences, you may remember moments of intense emotions when you would say "I was just speechless!" or "I just can't explain it to you!"

- Spirituality includes silence as an essential part of prayer and meditation. Subtle changes, sometimes life-transforming changes, can take place within us in silence.
- To enter the world of the spirit, it helps to acknowledge, trust, and value silence.

Trusting silence may be an uncomfortable challenge for those of us who were trained and deeply immersed in the world of science.

Reflections

If you want to move ahead in your spiritual quest, you will find it helpful to include thinking beyond denotation and literalism.

As you develop your capacity to hear the emotional connotations of the words people are using when talking to you, you will find rich, new depths of meaning in your relations with others. To respond to connotation requires both using your imagination and developing your capacity for empathy. You will find it helpful to give time and attention to listening with your heart!

I find that I can take in the contents of an equation very quickly. By staying with an equation, I can pull out both what it is saying and its implications. This process feels natural to me; I like its compactness and beauty. I can gain even more insight by displaying the equation graphically so that my visual intelligence can kick in.

Drawing out the meaning of a story narrative requires more effort and concentration on my part, but it has the power to reach me at a personal, deeper level. I energize my visualization of the narrative in my awareness of the emotional responses within me. I find I need to slow down and become more receptive, somewhat letting go of control. Learning to value and look for meanings other than the literal in a story has really enlarged my outlook in life and has produced very welcome growth in me as a person.

Exercises

Here are some useful exercises:

- What are some differences you experience between your work/technical education and your home/spiritual life cultures?
- Make a list of some metaphors you have used.
- List some symbols that you can relate to or feel touched by and some of the things they can stand for.

- Describe an incident in which a model in science or a software simulation package did not work.
- Give an example of literalism.
- Name a story you like, and find symbols and themes in it.
- Do you intentionally create a space for silence in your daily activities?
- Do you trust silence and acknowledge its worth?
- Read a short spiritual writing slowly and deliberately, looking for inward "tugs," points of personal resonance.
- How do you feel about living with ambiguity in spirituality?
- Take a story, read it literally, then read it again, looking for metaphors, symbols, and themes. Compare the results.

Chapter 3
A Common Ground

Introduction

I have loved science since I was a child. I built a ham radio station and a model rocket. My curiosity was very strong. Reading the life of Saint Francis really touched my life at that time. As I moved into adulthood, I was dismayed that these were actually two different worlds. Why is that so? Why aren't they under the same roof? This really puzzled me!

After so much has been printed in the past about the supposed conflicts between religion and science, it may come as a surprise to find out that they actually have several essential things in common! We need to move beyond clichés and soundbites! Let's review some fundamental concepts about the foundations of science and spirituality.

Figure 8 Common roots

54

The Universe

Western science finds its roots in the Jewish monotheistic religion and in the rational tradition of ancient Greece. The monotheism (belief in a single God) we inherited from the Jewish religion allows us to think of the large diversity of objects in the universe as having unity among themselves in spite of their obvious different locations and appearances. Newton used this concept when generalizing his idea of gravity on Earth as also applying to the rest of the universe.

Do you remember your very first physics textbook? This was probably your first exposure to the world of applied equations. I was told that these equations were expressions of the laws of nature and that physics would teach me these laws. The word *law* was used here to indicate that these rules were fixed and reliable. When I look back on the equations I learned in physics, at that time they seemed so dehumanized, distant, and cold. They made me think of a lawyer's office, the walls lined with shelves containing scores of law books with identical bindings.

Think of the great diversity of equations we encounter in physics: linear equations (Ohm's law), vectors (force), logarithms, trigonometric functions, exponentials, matrices, first and second derivatives, integrals, the Laplace and Fourier transforms, Maxwell's equations, Schrodinger's Wave Equation…What a huge variety of equations, each one displaying compactness, power, and beauty! Where did all these equations come from? Did they just pop up out of nowhere into a book of rules? I don't think so! All these rules are not only stored somewhere, waiting to be used, but these rules needed to be generated in the first place! These equations can be extremely sophisticated, requiring a wide variety of mathematical insights and tools. A high-enough intelligence is needed to create these rules and to enforce them. The rules of physics not only work individually, but are also harmonious with one another on a cosmic scale. Each rule exhibits the simplest form possible for achieving its purpose, covering terrains from the subatomic to the cosmic.

I personally don't find that the metaphor *natural law* is rich enough. It expresses reliability and constancy well but does nothing to show how the laws were created nor does it even attempt to explain the complexity of their contents and how they came to be in harmony with one another. I would say that this technical sophistication found throughout Nature has to come from a scientist, an artist, a creative mathematician with imagination and insight, possessing a sweeping panoramic vista of all. A metaphor that works better here for me personally would be *mind*. The Greek philosophers spoke of this metaphor, and they called it the *divine mind* or *the mind of the universe*. Please keep in mind that *mind* does not mean there is a large brain with exposed gray matter floating around in space somewhere! Remember that the word *mind* is used as a metaphor: we describe the unknown by identifying it with something similar that we are familiar with.

> The book of nature was written by God in the
> language of mathematics.
> —Galileo

The fact that these ideas come from ancient Greece doesn't mean we can undervalue them. Knowledge and insights don't decompose with age like foodstuff does! It's important to be aware of ethnocentric bias in ourselves that would make us reject something simply because it is old. We owe the existence of science to our Greek heritage.

- Science taps into this content of the Mind of the Universe in order to understand and predict how physical things work.

- Spirituality also acknowledges this Mind but goes one step further; it responds with gratitude for gifts received and seeks to find ways to express gratitude, giving love back for love received.

> Religion consists of the belief that there is an unseen order, and that our supreme good lies in harmoniously adjusting ourselves to it.
> —William James

Note: the physical universe following fixed rules does not carry over in its totality to living beings because they can exhibit purpose, self-initiative, and creativity that allows them to produce new things never before seen. They are not gears imprisoned in a mechanical clock.

After working for many years in different scattered fields of science and technology, it comes as a surprise to me that there is something common to all these vastly different fields. All the work I've done in science was always based on the universe being orderly enough to allow us to create technology. Being able to see all these different scattered parts of science as having something in common moves us up to a much higher plane, offering us a broader perspective of reality, an exhilarating, broad vision of a bigger picture.

Whether we realize it or not, when we do science, we are following the *mind of the universe*! I like this concept. It makes me think; I see things differently because of it. I learn to "see" beyond the limits of my senses. Both science and spirituality involve our determined efforts to move forward by observing patterns and then expressing them: in science, we seek to express these patterns in terms of data tables, flow charts, physical principles, or equations; in spirituality, we express our insights using metaphors, symbols, sacred narratives, and all the arts.

A common theme in many spiritual traditions is the need to develop a broader way of seeing reality, as if with a different eye. A challenge for us is to develop our ability to see with the "inner eye of love," open to beauty, loving relations, feeling love and compassion for all.

I Just Need to Know

It all begins with not knowing! There is no end to the things in our world that we don't know yet don't care about. On the other hand, there are other questions whose answers we don't know that produce a tension, a strong inner tugging within us, driving us, demanding that we find out the answers.

Jean Piaget (1896–1980) was a clinical psychologist who turned his professional skills to the observation of how children develop. Piaget's work laid a solid foundation for the field of child development studies. Piaget was struck by how relentlessly curious children are. He described children as "little scientists" because of their active, insatiable curiosity (Piaget 1964).

Curiosity comes from outside us. It's like a magnetic force that compels us to act; we just need to respond to it! As curiosity becomes stronger, all-encompassing, it can lead us into the experience of wonder. As we respond to wonder, we lose ourselves, the world outside vanishes, time stands still. We are totally caught up in the act of contemplating this new "wonder-full" thing: a blade of grass, a butterfly, a nebula, an elegant equation, an elegant flow chart, the workings of the human brain, the inside of a cell, the process of photosynthesis, the structure of a DNA helix…For me, science has allowed me to respond to this call to wonder, and I will never tire of it. It is an inseparable part of me; it feeds my soul!

Here is a possible sequence of events:

- Don't know: I don't know, and I accept that I don't know.
- Curiosity: I don't know, and yet I feel drawn into it. I can't help myself.
- I observe it: surprise, admiration.
- Wonder: Time stops. I am in the presence of something much bigger than myself. A relationship seems to call me. A sense of oneness! I want to share this with someone else!

Wonder is the emotion excited by perception of something novel and unexpected. Astonishment mingled with perplexity or bewildered curiosity. It often accompanies our perception of something that strikes us as intensely powerful, real, true, and or beautiful (Blackburn 1994).

Not knowing can be an invitation to curiosity, which can lead to wonder. As we follow the call of our sense of wonder, science allows us to describe what we are contemplating while simultaneously asking the question "How?" Science has empowered us to take this step. If we allow ourselves to go beyond the descriptive and number-based limitations of science (How?), we can then ask some of the many other questions ("Why?").

- Why was I invited? Who sent me the invitation?
- Why do I feel incomplete without knowing the answer?
- Why do I experience beauty? Where is the artist?

- Why do I see intricate, exquisitely engineered structures? Where is the architect/designer/engineer?
- Why have I received this present? Where is the gift giver?
- How can I respond to this loving gift?

Love all God's creation, the whole
and every grain of sand of it.
Love every leaf, every ray of God's light.
Love the animals, love the plants, love
everything.
If you love everything, you will perceive
the divine mystery in things.
Once you perceive it, you will begin
to comprehend it better every day.
And you will come at last to love the whole
world
with an all-embracing love.
—Fyodor Dostoyevsky

Childlike Sense of Wonder

I grew up loving art and nature. The search for God was very strong in me. I was touched as a teenager by reading the lives of Saint Francis and Mahatma Gandhi. I yearned to live life fully and intensely with God.

Moments in my life when I experienced a great sense of wonder and mystery:

- As a small boy crawling on hands and knees in the backyard: absorbed, looking at ants mysteriously walking between the blades of grass and mysteriously going in and out of a hole in the ground.

- My chemistry set: watching chemical reactions take place with changing colors, bubbles, and smells...
- Building a simple radio and listening to extremely weak human voices (?) magically coming out over the headphones.
- Building a ham radio station, learning Morse code. Communicating with people in other countries. Modifying my circuit wiring, then seeing my ham radio transmitter go up in a mushroom cloud of smoke!
- Building a model rocket from scratch (which exploded on me and quickly cured me of ever wanting to continue in that area).

I was always taking things apart to see how they worked. My poor mom would arrive home after a hard day at work to discover that the apartment was totally dark because I had burned out all the fuses, or she would find our toaster or a mechanical clock all taken apart with screws and gears all over the kitchen table, never to function again!

A child's world is fresh and new and beautiful, full of

Figure 9 Rachel Carson

wonder and excitement. It is our misfortune that for most of us that clear-eyed vision, that true instinct for what is beautiful and awe—inspiring, is dimmed and even lost before we reach adulthood. If I had influence with the good fairy who is supposed to preside over the christening of all children I should ask that her gift to each child in the world be a sense of wonder so indestructible that it would last throughout life, as an unfailing antidote against the boredom and disenchantments of later years, the sterile preoccupation with things that are artificial, the alienation from the sources of our strength (Carson 1965).

Science feeds our curiosity, our childlike sense of wonder, our search for beauty, belonging, love, unity. As we are entering into mystery, we can sometimes unwittingly terminate this process by categorizing what we see:

Figure 10 Dandelion

"Dandelion: Taraxacum is a large genus of flowering plants in the family Asteraceae and consists of species commonly known as dandelion. They are native to. Eurasia and North America, and two species, *T. officinale* and *T. erythrospermum*, are found as commonplace wild flowers worldwide. Both species are edible in their entirety" (Wikipedia).

We can be fooled into thinking we have exhausted the meaning of that dandelion by following a strict adherence to categories of mass, energy, time, chemistry, and equations. Naming (Name?) is not enough; describing (How?) is not enough! To enter more deeply into mystery (Why? Who?) requires our opening ourselves up to include our emotions and our capacity for loving relationships. At this point we can transition to the languages of spirituality: art, love, beauty, poetry, and silence.

> I know not what I may appear to the world, but to myself I seem to have been only like a boy playing on the seashore, and diverting myself in now and then finding a smoother pebble or a prettier shell than ordinary, whilst the great ocean of truth lay all undiscovered before me.
>
> —Sir Isaac Newton

> Truly I tell you, unless you change and become like children, you will never enter the kingdom of heaven.
>
> —Matthew 18:3

> And a little child shall lead them
>
> —Isaiah 11:6

> The most beautiful experience we can have is the mysterious. It is the fundamental emotion which stands at the cradle of true art and true science. Whoever does not know it and can no longer wonder, no longer marvel, is as good as dead, and his eyes are dimmed.
>
> —Albert Einstein

Aristotle saw wonder as the highest reach of mind: the rational mood par excellence, the mood of earnest receptivity and active search for truth. He saw it as a mood in the precise sense that it is not a thought but is a way of thinking and feeling. In this regard it is like beauty, a way of thinking and feeling, with which it shares important qualities. For Aristotle, wonder lay in a world just out of the mind's reach. "It was through the feeling of wonder," wrote Aristotle, "that men now and at first began to philosophize" (Sandelands and Carlsen 2013, 306).

> In all things of nature there is something of the marvelous.
>
> —Aristotle

Robert C. Fuller (Fuller 2006) has studied the terrain of wonder. There are five known ways that can bring on the experience of wonder: art, love, scientific investigation, experiencing nature, and religion. Human beings worldwide for the last 100,000 years have been using religion as a means of getting in touch with their natural sense of wonder.

The experience of wonder is beyond words yet true. Wonder feels right; no one has to justify it to us. There is a sense of arriving at the right place. There is a sense of returning home, our true home, of experiencing something only dimly remembered. The experience of wonder is expansive. It enlarges our mind to new vistas and, more importantly, to relationship with the source of wonder, the person behind the mystery, and with people around us.

> For this is an experience which is characteristic of a philosopher, this wondering; this is where philosophy begins and nowhere else.
>
> —Socrates

Awe

After I had spent many years studying to be an engineer, followed by many more years practicing my engineering skills, I decided to take a nighttime beginning course in biology at a local community college. Upon first opening my textbook to a page showing the inner components of a living cell, I had a very powerful experience of awe. *Wow!* I have never forgotten that experience. At that time, I was working on the highest-level complexity known of large-scale integrated semiconductor systems. As I attempted to take in the absolute awesomeness of the cell, I was truly overwhelmed and humbled. My technical work all of a sudden seemed so small, stiff, and limited in comparison to the majesty of one single cell!

The exhilarating experience of *Aha!* is what keeps us all going ahead in our technical work in spite of many failures and reversals along the way. There is a beautiful awe to discovering new insights in science. It is a great thrill to design a system and to then see it work after all our efforts. Awe cannot be contained. Awe has a sweet, luminous, expansive quality to it. It bewilders us. It overwhelms our senses. It is contagious; it calls us to share our discoveries with others, even with strangers.

I now believe that the search for order in the universe is part of our hunger for God. Intelligence, beauty, creativity, all these are attributes of God. Science lets us have a breathtaking glimpse of some of this beauty, a glimpse that can leave us bewildered. I believe that the universe displays the great works of God. By contemplating these wonders, we satisfy some of our yearning for God.

Yahweh, our Lord,
how great your name throughout the earth!
Above the heavens is your Majesty chanted
by the mouths of children, babes in arms.
I look up at your heavens, made by your
fingers,
at the moon and stars, you set in place—
ah, what is man that you should spare a
thought for him.

—Psalm 8

The heavens declare the glory of God,
the vault of heaven proclaims his handiwork;
day discourses of it today,
night to night hands on the knowledge.

—Psalm 19

Respecting the Truth as Being Larger Than Myself

Continued experimental work can have a sobering effect on us if we are open to what we observe. We realize that nature has not read any of our books or attended any of our conferences, and it does not feel beholden to behave in a way expected by us. This is a humbling experience. We learn that truth is hard to come by. We need to be ready to put aside our preconceptions and be open to what may be in front of us. As we humans have experienced great upheavals in our belief systems throughout the course of history, truth keeps flowing steadily across these human barriers.

Sit down before fact as a little child, be prepared to give up every preconceived notion, follow humbly wherever and to whatsoever abysses Nature leads, or you shall learn nothing.

—Thomas Henry Huxley

An open-mindedness and a willingness to accept correction to our preconceptions are required both in research and in the practice of spirituality. This attitude can be of great help when we are facing very difficult times of personal decision making. Putting our emotions and preconceptions aside and staying open to events as they unfold can be very helpful in facing some life crises. The practice of passionate indifference consists of always maintaining a passion for the truth yet staying open to whatever the results of our research may be, staying open to self-examination.

Truth experienced has a transcendent quality to it. Truth is not swayed by fashion and expectations; it does its own thing. This *Aha!* experience is what drives much of research work.

Both Active and Receptive

Figure 11 Thomas Alva Edison

Genius consists of 1 percent inspiration and
99 percent perspiration.

—Thomas Alva Edison

If there was ever a person whose down-to-earth practical accomplishments have transformed our modern society, it was Edison. Edison's wise remark, which was based on his lengthy experience as a prolific inventor who earned more than a thousand patents, forewarns us that, in order to attain a technical goal, it is necessary to intentionally utilize not one, but two distinct modes of problem solving. In practice, these two modes are not neatly compartmentalized; they become intertwined in our day-to-day struggles. We need to use both the receptive/passive (1 percent inspiration) and the controlling/active (99 percent perspiration) modes. This insight turns out to be true of both working in science and working on our spiritual growth.

Our education in science has mostly emphasized the 99 percent perspiration part of solving a problem: being in control, staying focused and analytical, making conscious decisions, pushing hard. In this mode, we feel that we are acting alone and we are fully responsible for actively solving the problem. We believe that our success will come about based on our efforts and our efforts only.

Missing from our education has been the receptive (1 percent inspiration) part: staying passive, expectant, being spontaneous, trusting in the process, being open to receiving a gift, intuitive, using our imagination, staying open ended. "All of a sudden, I saw the solution; it came to me out of nowhere!" Since we do not personally create inspiration, it has to come from somewhere other than us, from a wiser, broader, more creative mind than ours: the mind of God.

> If we compare how great scientific ideas arrive, they look remarkably like religious revelation viewed in a non—mystical way.
> —Charles H. Townes
> Nobel Prize–winning physicist

> There is no logical way to the discovery of elemental laws. There is only the way of intuition, which is helped by a feeling for the order lying behind the appearance.
> —Albert Einstein

> The intuitive mind is a sacred gift and the rational mind is a faithful servant. We have created a society that honors the servant and has forgotten the gift.
> —Albert Einstein

Our spirituality, in order to remain balanced and fruitful, also needs to include both inspiration and perspiration. Inspiration can't be forced; we can't demand that it happen. Inspiration can take place when we let go of control, when we develop a spirit, an attitude, of openness and expectancy, having faith that a gift will be received. Passivity, openness, and trust in the process are essential for inspiration to take place. Inspiration is truly a gift received. Inspiration gives us guidance; at the same time, it can establish and reinforce in us a loving, trusting relationship with God, who is the source of all inspiration.

There is no true spirituality that does not also include perspiration: struggling with our self-knowledge, overcoming our compulsions, our self-defeating beliefs and behaviors, participating in compassionately and actively helping our suffering brothers and sisters.

- Developing an awareness of the environment we live in and its needs. We live in a deeply hurting world with poverty, great injustices, human loneliness, and dehumanization in general. It takes a lot of hard work to go against these trends.
- Acquiring self-knowledge in some depth. Identifying our talents and potentials. Identifying our underdeveloped, hurting, and hurtful parts. Self-knowledge is a lifelong task requiring openness, humility, and a lot of hard work.
- Developing deep caring relationships with those around us. It takes effort and patience to move out of our self-centeredness.
- Taking an active part in responding to the needs of people around us.

Let's contrast two different ways of relating to something in the external world.

1. External, controlled by effort: When I'm going to perform an experiment, set up instruments, read a technical report, write some software, or fix a technical problem, I am at that time relating to an object, an instrument, a flowchart, a report, or a computer. I am trying to extract information from this object, I try to control the environment as much as I can, and I take in information at my bidding.

2. Spontaneous, received as gift: All of a sudden, a solution to a technical problem "just comes to me unexpectedly." As I'm driving home, all of a sudden, I'm struck by the fact that there is a beautiful sunset taking place. As I am interacting with someone, all of a sudden, I begin to experience within me a call to a deeper friendship or perhaps even love. As I'm listening to music something stirs within me that comes from my depths.

- In the first case, the key is that I am the one who initiates the transaction; I control the transaction as much as possible. This process is goal driven.

- In the second case, I'm not in control. Something outside me is gifting me with this experience; my task is to remain open, appreciative, and receptive to the gift.

Beauty

Have you ever stopped to think what it would be like if we lived in a purely functional universe? The universe certainly could have been functional without being beautiful. Beauty is superfluous, not needed for functionality at all. Picture all the birds looking essentially the same except for size, a standardized shape, their coloring perhaps some variations of khaki brown.

71

We can unwittingly take for granted all that goes beyond mere functionality found in nature:

- Graceful motion: the flight of a snowy white egret, the mating dance of the blue-footed booby.
- Colors: the rainbow, butterflies, flowers, nebulae, peacocks, crystal structures.
- Textures: lamb fleece, wet grass, rain, rivulets of water.
- Music, song: the warble of a singing bird.
- Love, commitment: penguins taking care of their baby penguin.
- Architectural design, sculpture: a spider web, a beehive.
- Resourcefulness, ingenuity, elegance, simplicity of functional design: the desert rat, which generates crystallized urine to conserve water.

> Consider the lilies, how they grow: they neither toil nor spin, yet I tell you, even Solomon in all his glory was not clothed like one of these.
>
> Luke 11:27

> Beauty is the gift of God.
> —Aristotle

As I look out my window, I can see a beautiful sunrise unfolding. The contrasting swirling colors and textures, the rhythm and grace of its spreading motion, all fill me with a great sense of beauty. I think of my outdoors activities, my gardening over many years, the great love I have for all forms of art.

When we are at the beach or in a forest, we may discover a beautiful rock, a seashell, a small flower, a beautiful piece of driftwood. As we are filled by its beauty, we cannot contain it; it can't help but overflow our souls. We are driven to turn to another person and say, "Look, look at this, see how beautiful!" In my imagination, I picture that when God the artist created sea shells, shiny rocks, and small flowers, the experience of beauty was so overwhelmingly expansive that God had to call to us through our sense of wonder and say "Look, look, see how beautiful!" Beauty leads to wonder that needs to be shared and can create a loving bond between those who now can share that experience.

Reflecting on my experience of beauty, I realize that this treasure I so cherish is mine prior to and independent of my love and commitment to the field of science. I could have experienced beauty without ever having a background in science at all. The ability to experience beauty is not elitist but innate, universal, open to all people. The experience of beauty can exist totally outside the range of science, yet my knowing science can enhance my appreciation for the complex, beautiful, and graceful order that is found in nature.

Within the work of science, beauty can provide initial motivation, insight, and guidance. It is very telling that what motivated Copernicus to reject the Ptolemaic system with its epicycles was that it was ugly, messy, "monstrous." It did not exhibit the beauty of the divine mind as was to be expected. Copernicus wanted to derive a model of the world machine worthy of its creator, whom he called "the best and most orderly workman of all." As far as Copernicus was concerned, Ptolemy's system was too messy to have been designed by God (Hannam 2000, 277).

I have a friend who's an artist and has sometimes taken a view which I don't agree with very well. He'll hold up a flower and say "look how beautiful it is," and I'll agree. Then he says "I as an artist can see how beautiful this is but you as a scientist take this all apart and it becomes a dull thing," and I think that he's kind of nutty. First of all, the beauty that he sees is available to other people and to me too, I believe…I can appreciate the beauty of a flower. At the same time, I see much more about the flower than he [his artist friend] sees. I could imagine the cells in there, the complicated actions inside, which also have a beauty. I mean it's not just beauty at this dimension, at one centimeter; there's also beauty at smaller dimensions, the inner structure, also the processes...It adds a question: does this aesthetic sense also exist in the lower forms? Why is it aesthetic? All kinds of interesting questions which the science knowledge only adds to the excitement, the mystery and the awe of a flower. It only adds. I don't understand how it subtracts.

—Richard Feynman
"Ode to the Flower"
1965 Nobel Peace Prize in physics

Does the world embody beautiful ideas?...The answer to this question is a resounding Yes! The most daring hopes of Pythagoras and Plato to find conceptual purity, order, and harmony at the heart of creation have been far exceeded by reality. There really is a Music of the Spheres embodied in atoms and the modern Void, not unrelated to music in the ordinary sense, but adding a strangeness and abundance all its own. The Solar System does not embody Kepler's original vision, but he himself discovered the precision of dynamical laws, and thus enabled the transcendent beauty of Newtonian of celestial mechanics. There really is much more to light even than our wondrous sense of vision reveals, and our imagination—and not only our imagination! — opens new Doors of Perception. The basic forces of nature embody symmetry, and are implemented by its avatars.

—Frank Wilczek
Nobel Prize in physics, 2004

The scientist does not study nature because it is useful to do so. He studies it because he takes pleasure in it; and he takes pleasure in it because it is beautiful. If nature were not beautiful, it would not be worth knowing, and life would not be worth living...I mean the intimate beauty which comes from the harmonious order of its parts and which a pure intelligence can grasp.

—Henrí Poincaré
Mathematician and physicist

I thank thee, Lord God our Creator, that thou allowest me to see the beauty in thy work of Creation.

—Johannes Kepler

Mathematics is the archetype of the beauty of the world.

—Johannes Kepler

Beauty is one of those rare things that does not lead to doubt of God.

—Jean Arnouilh

All forms of beauty, like all possible phenomena, contain an element of the eternal and an element of the transitory—of the absolute and of the particular.

—Charles Baudelaire

We ascribe beauty to that which is simple; which has no superfluous parts; which exactly answers its end; which stands related to all things; which is the mean of many extremes.

—Ralph Waldo Emerson

Beauty is the translucence, through the material phenomenon, of the eternal splendor of the ONE.

—Plotinus

Beauty is the splendor of truth.

—Latin motto

Beauty is the proper conformity of the parts to one another and to the whole.

—Werner Heisenberg

The beauty of creatures is nothing other than an image of the divine beauty in which things participate.

—St. Thomas Aquinas

Art pales when compared to the workings of nature.

—St. Thomas Aquinas

Somehow the idea of art and aesthetics and beauty underlies all of the scientific work I do. Whatever I do, I try to do it in a way that has some elegance; I try to create something that I think is beautiful.

—Donald E. Knuth
Author of The Art of Computer Programming
and winner of the 1974 Alan Turing Award

Science without religion is lame, religion without science is blind.

—Albert Einstein

Spirituality originally set the foundation for science by proclaiming the divine mind (unity, intelligibility, orderliness) of the universe. Science and spirituality share many values: curiosity, wonder, awe, love of beauty, use of reason, faith in a positive outcome, effort, tenacity, determination, and dogged persistence in the search for the truth.

Science and spirituality can share a common quest for a deeper experience of mystery. Scientists are well known for their passion for truth, their discipline, tenacity, energy, and commitment to reach their goals in better understanding the patterns (How?) underlying the physical universe. Science seeks to derive physical principles, to express these via equations, and to then use them in solving practical problems. Besides this, the results of scientific research can also give us insights into our place in the universe.

Spirituality seeks a deeper knowledge of and relationship with God by entering into the realm of mystery and then expressing these insights (Why?) via metaphors, symbols, sacred stories, and art.

Science can provide us with a tremendous power to change our physical universe. Simultaneously, spirituality can provide us with a sense of cosmic meaning, with ethical guidance in using our knowledge with compassion and wisdom while enhancing beauty. When science and spirituality work together, they can bring about much-needed change in our world. Our world is faced with severe issues that are inextricably both technical and spiritual:

- Worldwide environmental problems
- Large-scale ethnic violence
- Scarcity of resources
- The staggering weight of sheer numbers of populations
- Massive unemployment
- Waves of displaced refugee families
- Addiction and its associated devastating effects
- Dehumanization in general
- The loss of face-to-face accountability of institutions
- Human trafficking of the powerless
- Oppression of people

We need to work together to make our world a better world!

A Survey of Scientists

Sociologist Elaine Howard Ecklund carried out an extensive study of the religious beliefs of scientists. She collected data from 2005 to 2008. Technical disciplines that were contacted included physicists, chemists, biologists, sociologists, political scientists, and psychologists. The researcher observed that there was very little difference between natural and social scientists in their religious propensities (Ecklund 2010, 10).

Questionnaires were mailed out to 1,700 scientists, then later followed by one-on-one interviews with 275 of the original respondents.

Here is a list of the universities included in the study: Columbia University, Cornell University, Duke University, Harvard University, Johns Hopkins University, Massachusetts Institute of Technology, Princeton University, Stanford University, University of Pennsylvania, University of California at Berkeley, University of California Los Angeles, University of Chicago, University of Illinois Urbana Champaign, University of Michigan Ann Arbor, University of Minnesota Twin Cities, University of North Carolina Chapel Hill, University of Washington Seattle, University of Wisconsin Madison, University of Southern California, Washington University, and Yale University.

Ecklund found out that 47 percent of the scientists studied had religious traditions, compared to 84 percent of the general public (Ecklund 2010, 16).

According to Ecklund, the four most typical reasons given by scientists for staying away from religion were as follows:

1. Because science trumps religion

This group believes that in all spheres of life, only knowledge that is found through science is reliable. Likewise, for them, only questions answerable through science are worth exploring (scientism). Questions concerning the meaning of life are not even worth asking. (p. 17).

2. Because religion has let them down

How can a good God allow bad things to happen? (p., 22).

Memories of negative personal experiences with their religious traditions of their past (p. 23).

3. Because religion is foreign or unimportant

"About 13 percent of scientists were raised in homes with no religious tradition…Nearly 87 percent of scientists whose families were part of a religious tradition, membership was sometimes only significant as a label rather than a matter of regular practice" (p, 25).

4. Fear of ridicule from peers

"The scientists I talked to are among the most educated people in our society…when it comes to talking about matters of faith, they often have a restricted [language] code [vocabulary and ways of talking] based on shorthand stereotypes. In other words, they are not articulate. Thus, they might lump all religion into fundamentalism, or discredit religious claims based on premature assumptions. And because most elite scientists have limited interactions with religious people who share their views about science, the stereotypes persist" (p., 27).

Personal Reflections

I have always loved beauty as found in art, nature, and people. I have likewise also loved science. It has come as a surprise

79

to me to see so many scientists over the ages stating that beauty was important to them in their work. I now feel closer to these gifted people I have always admired. The centuries and the miles that separate us are no longer barriers. I pledge to myself to always do my best to keep alive and joyful my childlike sense of curiosity. I pledge to myself to consciously keep my sense of wonder alive!

- The Mind of the Universe provides us with a common source, an all-pervasive bedrock connection between science and spirituality.

- Beauty can provide a very tight joining of science and spirituality.

- The fallacy of describing. I want to break with the illusion that naming, describing the physical properties of something, or categorizing it means I now fully understand this or relate to it.

Reflections

- Do you feel there is yet an untapped part of life calling you? Do you yearn for a fuller, richer enjoyment and awareness of life? If so, read on!

- Why did you decide to major in science?

- What ignites your curiosity, your sense of wonder?

- What do you do to open yourself to wonder?

- Recall any *Aha!* moments of new insight you've experienced in your technical work.

- Have you ever felt gripped by an experience greater than yourself?

- Recall any moments in your life when you felt drawn by mystery.
- Recall moments when you experienced beauty, beauty that needed to be shared with someone else.
- Recall special moments of experiencing art.
- What have been special moments for you in experiencing nature?
- What do you do to keep past experiences of beauty, wonder, or awe alive in your life today?
- What special experiences have you had in a close relationship with another person?

For Further Reading

Cootsona, Gregory S. 2011. "How Nature and Beauty Can Bring Scientists and Theologians Together." *Theology and Science* 9(4): 384.

Wilber, Ken, ed. 2001. *Quantum Questions: Mystical Writings of the World's Greatest Physicists*. Boston: Shambhala Publications, Inc.

[Beauty] Theology and Science, Vol 11, No 3, August 2013.

Hemenway, Priya. 2005. *Divine Proportion: Phi in Art, Nature, and Science*. New York: Sterling Publishing Co.

Skinner, Stephen. 2006. *Sacred Geometry: Deciphering the Code*. New York: Sterling Publishing Company.

Huntley, H. E. 1970. *The Divine Proportion: A Study in Mathematical Beauty*. Mineola, NY: Dover Publications.

DuBay, Thomas S. M. 1999. *The Evidential Power of Beauty*. San Francisco: Ignatius Press.

Wilczek, Frank. 2015. *A Beautiful Question: Finding Nature's Deep Design*. New York: Viking.

Chapter 4
Some Limitations of Science

There's no question about it: science has a fantastic track record! Over the last three centuries, science has shown an impressive ability to predict the behavior of our physical world, eventually leading to its control through technology. Science surely deserves to be granted the halo effect, the expectation that someone who has impressed us by his or her performance in the past will surely, without question, also perform well always and can be trusted to be right (Thorndike 1920, 25–9).

The long list of accomplishments of science raises the obvious question: Can science do all? If the answer is yes, we could, in principle, eliminate all other forms of education. Gone would be programs in literature, arts, humanities, philosophy, religion, and intercultural and interpersonal relations. Visualizing the resulting scenario and reflecting on it suggests that this would be a disaster! The answer to the original question needs to be evaluated in some detail. Not every one of our pressing everyday problems or our long-term vision can be resolved using science! What else is it that we need?

We entered the twentieth century with unbounded optimism about what science could do. As we started to probe into the subatomic dimension, we were shocked to find out that it did not behave the same way as the visible world around us did. Also, the Heisenberg uncertainty principle taught us that we cannot just refine our measuring instruments more and more; rather, there is an essential limitation to all measurements. We likewise learned that there is a limit to our ability to observe nature. Science has run into essential limitations within its own domains of matter, space, and energy. Modern physics has reintroduced the attitudes of unknowing, paradox, and mystery into our observation of the physical universe.

The Only Source of Truth

The power and scope of science is so impressive that it's very easy to conclude that it can do all: that all matters of truth and falsehood can be authoritatively determined by science. Can science always tell me what is true and what is not true? Let's review some facts of logic. Look at the following statement:

"This sentence is false."

The sentence as it stands tells me that it is false. Thus, if the statement is true, it is false. This leaves us in unsettled confusion. This sentence is known in the discipline of logic as a self-refuting statement; it resolves nothing!

Now let's look at another sentence:

"Only that which can be proven through science is true."

Since there is no experiment we can perform to test the validity of that sentence, it must be false by its own wording. We would say that this sentence is also a self-refuting sentence. It resolves nothing; it carries no weight. When trying to decide whether something is true or false, we require access to other tools besides the scientific experiment.

Conducting an Experiment

I have done experimental work for many years during my career. Below is a list of elements of the scientific method that I have encountered repeatedly. They are not necessarily in order since we typically may have to cycle through them a few times.

Since the original success of Galileo's work, a very large number of many other disciplines have attempted to emulate his approach but may have had to make adaptations appropriate to their field, giving to the word *"science"* a variety of meanings. Feel free to adapt the following steps as necessary.

Inspiration: Conceptualize, use imagination, intuition, visualization.

Strategy: Plan and set goals.

Anticipate: Set up instrumentation ahead of time.

Isolate: Make sure that outside factors won't affect the data being measured.

Control: Change only one variable at a time in order to observe a resulting change in the quantity being measured.

Observe: Measure using instruments.

Simplify: Start with the simplest model possible.

Numbers: Deal with numbers.

Bounded: Valid data is bounded from below and from above by the instruments used.

Patterns: Look for patterns in the data collected.

Repeat: Anyone should be able to repeat your results.

Generalize Results: Generalize the specific data as being universal. All results will have to be tentative.

Scientism

Ever since the 1600s, science has opened to us vast amounts of knowledge of the material world that grant us the power to control nature. We live in an age of technology when new accomplishments follow one after another after another. There seems to be no limit to what technology can do! This is the spirit of our age. The great success of the physical sciences over the last three centuries has given birth to a widespread cultural phenomenon known as scientism.

Scientism gives a fully exclusive value to science as a means of knowing all. It says that all can ultimately be known by science and besides, that science is the only valid way of knowing. Scientism has eventually taken on the role of a basic belief system, one that we hold internally without necessarily even being aware of its presence, since most aspects of one's culture are learned through observation and imitation, rather than by explicit verbal instruction or expression (Samovar and Porter 2000, 211). A basic belief system is usually held unconsciously, it has a "knee-jerk" quality to it.

> "Science says," will generally be found to settle any argument in a social gathering, or sell any article from toothpaste to refrigerators.
>
> —*The Nation* (1928)

Throughout my life, I have drifted in and out of at least five different levels of personally identifying with scientism. Here is a list of these beliefs, followed by my present-day reaction to each of them. I am also including my global personal reflections at the end. I strongly suggest that you spend time reflecting on your personal response to each one of these five beliefs systems and see their impact on you.

1. If something could not be proven by science, I was not interested in it.

This attitude led to my neither acknowledging nor valuing the efforts, knowledge, and accomplishments of my nontechnical friends. I unconsciously felt superior to others. I had developed selective attention to the world and was losing some of my curiosity and spontaneity.

I personally like to observe a small child on a playground with his or her boundless energy: constantly moving, jumping, reaching, taking things apart, peeking in, lifting up, looking around, looking behind, crawling under: constantly, with great joy, moving outside the "box" of its present limited life experience.

Our individual human cycles of growth from childhood to old age and death consist of a long series of developmental boxes that we must grow into and then later move out of sequentially, over and over again, as we mature. Our developmental life-cycle boxes give us safety in which to grow until we are ready to move on to the next box.

Recorded human history shows bursts of new forward motion occurring only when someone could think outside the box. The scientific revolution is a good example of the difficulty that had been created by the importance given to Aristotelian philosophy and a literal interpretation of scripture at that time and how difficult it was to move beyond its methods. The spirit of the scientific revolution was meant to teach us not just that its immediate results in astronomy should replace one box with another, but a broader lesson of the importance of always staying open to new ways of seeing.

In the present, I make a pledge to myself from now on to always make room to listen to voices that may come from outside my present box. I want to be open to growth, surprise, and freshness. It's important for grownups to always stay open to the excitement of peeking outside the box, so that the box doesn't become a substitute for reality.

Unless you become like little children, you
will never enter the Kingdom of God.
—Matthew 18:3

2. If something could not be decided by science, I didn't know if I could make a decision about it.

During my formative years in engineering college, I grew to understand and trust science more and more, not realizing that, very unobtrusively, as I valued science more and more, I was simultaneously growing to value other forms of problem solving and my subjective self less and less. As I entered more deeply into my engineering studies, the great aura of the authority of science was creating in me a spirit of expecting science to make decisions for me. A weakening of part of my decision-making ability was taking place, coupled with an almost exclusive reliance on science for problem solving. This attitude was threatening to bring me in and out of a constant state of indecision and agnosticism, stuck without being able to move forward.

Literally from birth to death, life relentlessly thrusts the inescapable burden of decision making on us over and over again: meaning versus despair, self-love versus self-hatred, engagement versus passivity, loving relatedness versus isolation, growth versus stagnation, creativity versus predictability, forgiveness versus revenge, and so on. No escaping! Not to decide is itself a decision. Life is too precious to be wasted; it demands from us that we respond with decisive action to all important issues facing us.

Howard Gardner has identified eight different forms of human intelligence. (See chapter 5.) If our analytic mode of intelligence cannot totally resolve a problem facing us, it is important to include some of the other seven modes of human intelligence as well. When the totality of our education and a large percentage of our daily work exclusively challenge our analytical mode, our other modes of intelligence can become neglected, requiring us to make a conscious effort to acknowledge, trust, and develop them.

> Openness to experience means lack of rigidity and permeability of boundaries and concepts, beliefs, perceptions, and hypotheses. It means a tolerance for ambiguity where ambiguity exists. It means the ability to receive much conflicting information without forcing closure upon the situation (Rogers 1961).

Saying that I cannot reach a decision regarding a problem utilizing only science, and therefore can't act, is not an acceptable answer!

In the present, I consciously try to access all my modes of problem solving, not just analytical, at different times as needed, in order to respond to the challenges facing me at that moment.

3. If something could not be proven by science, I could be certain that it was false.

Our past and present lives are filled with deeply significant moments whose meaning cannot be proven by science yet cannot be ignored. Science is a wonderful tool, but it possesses only a limited range of usefulness. A good workbench will contain a wide variety of tools of different sizes, shapes, and applications.

In the present, I realize that I need to use judgment in selecting which tool or combination of tools to use at any time while resisting the temptation to use the same familiar tool for all applications.

4. I used to believe that science would eventually answer all my questions.

At the beginning of the twentieth century, some people were predicting that science would eventually answer all our questions. In 1894, the physicist Albert A. Michelson, said "The more important fundamental laws and facts of physical science have all been discovered, and they're now so firmly established that the possibility of them ever been supplanted in consequence of new discoveries is exceedingly remote." Also, in 1900, speaking to the British Association for the Advancement of Science, Lord Kelvin said "There's nothing new to be discovered in physics now. All that remains is more and more precise measurements" (Sacks 2011, 272).

The models that we use in science are known ahead of time to be limited in their application. All instruments used for measurement can function only over a limited range of values. A lower bound to all measurements is set by the noise levels present and by the instrument's sensitivity and resolution. An upper limit to measurements is set by the instrument's linear range of operation. Instrumentation bandwidth, response time, memory size, speed of computation, and long-term stability also create limits to our ability to carry out measurements. Some very large software programs already have reached the complexity levels at which they cannot be tested for all combinations of input values. For the above reasons, I now realize that all our models used in science can be experimentally verified only over a limited range of values.

> As the circle of light increases, so does the circumference of darkness.
>
> —Albert Einstein
> (Attributed)

The more we learn about the world, the deeper our learning, the more conscious, specific and articulate will be our knowledge of what we do not know, our knowledge of our ignorance.

—Karl Popper
Philosopher of Science

The last function of reason is to recognize
that there is an infinity of things which are
beyond it. It is but feeble if it does not see so
far as to know this.

—Blaise Pascal
Philosopher, Mathematician, Scientist

5. This is my present conscious choice.

Limitations notwithstanding, I want to stay joyfully and
expectantly open to the larger world, both inside and outside
science, receptive to other modes of thinking and valuing. I am
strongly committed to living intensely, while using my critical
judgment as to which combination of tools is appropriate for me to
use at any given time.

Given that science is not enough, what are some of its
important outer boundaries?

Measurement Results Can Be Expressed by Using Numbers

The essential core and foundation of the physical sciences is
undoubtedly mathematics, which is the language of numbers, their
patterns, and the relationships between them. Science's total
identification with mathematics gives it both its strength and its
weakness. Science is strong because of the clarity of the language of
mathematics and its ability to model physical processes in the
universe with insightful elegance, compactness, and precision.
Simultaneously, science is weak because it excludes itself
automatically by its association with mathematics when faced with

91

issues that are not describable by numbers. Generally speaking, issues involving meaning (as in the meaning of life), moral right or wrong, beauty, love, and our human inner world are all excluded from the scope of number-based science. When we reflect on our lived life experiences, we will see that these nonnumerical issues are the very stuff of which the human drama is woven. Obviously, to live life consciously and to the fullest, it is important that we broaden our vision to look elsewhere in order to capture the richness of these essential elements of life.

> Mathematics is the door and the key to the sciences.
> —Francis Bacon
> Opus Majus, 1267

> If you can measure that of which you speak, and can express it by a number, you know something of your subject; but if you cannot measure it, your knowledge is meager and unsatisfactory.
> —William Thomas, Lord Kelvin
> British physicist (1824–1907)

Some practical limitations of science:

"When solving some differential equations, small differences in the coefficients can lead to very large, chaotic differences in results of a computation (chaos) such as in weather prediction, the three-body problem, stock market, epidemiology, biological population studies, fluids. Chaotic systems have shown that the Newtonian dream of calculating the future of every system is over. Laplace's optimism was for naught; the universe is far more complicated than he thought" (Yanofsky 2013, 162- 166).

Our modeling equations are imperfect metaphors, approximations of only a limited range of reality. They are not identical to what they attempt to describe.

- The map is not the road.
- The finger pointing at the moon is not the moon.
- The model is not identical to the thing it models.
- The metaphor is not the same as what it stands for.

Data Can Be Observed

This component of science requires that the data be observable through the senses or through their extension using instruments.

Observing something cannot take place spontaneously at our whim. The act of observing requires sufficient advance notice, funding, facilities with a controllable and isolated environment, specialized equipment, trained personnel, plus considerable advance strategizing and calculations.

When I was doing my doctoral research, the experimental verification of my theoretical predictions involved an experiment that took three hours to carry out. However, to perform that three-hour experiment required literally thousands of hours spent over a three-year period doing literature searches, some 1,200 pages of lab notes with detailed calculations, instrument selection and setup, many abortive measurements, and so on. Observing something through science exhibits the obvious problems of advance planning, inertia, cost, and a lack of flexibility. It's obvious we cannot do this during the course of our day-to-day living.

Besides the issues of cost and lack of flexibility, we also face a more fundamental problem in that our inner world—our emotions, our memory of past life events, imagination, intuitions, and the creative process—cannot be readily observed externally or reduced to numerical values.

We should place great value on our inner world. It is an all-powerful, essential, and distinctive part of who we are. The scientific method, which is natural for working with numerical physics problems, will not carry over into trying to identify our inner world. It is essential for our well-being and personal growth that we develop an ongoing relationship with our inner world. To accomplish this requires turning to the same tools used in the language of spirituality: metaphor, story, symbol, theme, personal associations, and connotations.

The Use of Induction

In science, a common way of gaining new knowledge is to take data from experiments performed, review this, and then work to develop general statements about it. We are going from the specific to the universal. This is called induction.

Induction is going from observing many single instances to a general rule...The problem of induction is at the very core of science. Scientific laws are formulated by taking measurements and then generalizing them to universal rules which we call laws of nature. There are, however, no real reasons why we have the right to come up with such generalizations.

The law that Newton gave us that describes the motion of pairs of bodies was not formulated because Newton examined all pairs of bodies in the universe. Rather he formulated the law by using understanding and induction on what he saw. In fact, the law is simply false when applied to all pairs of objects. Quantum mechanics have shown us that subatomic particles do not follow Newton's simple law.

General relativity has also shown that Newton's laws are not the whole story.

We conclude that Newton's laws were formulated with induction and they turned out to be false [when generalized]. They do not work for very small or very large objects, as revealed to us by the physics revolution of the 20th century" (Yanofsky 2013, 237).

The use of the word *law* raises an interesting question: What does this so-familiar word mean? Human laws can be broken. We can drive (carefully) through a red light. Human laws are arbitrary. One country requires we drive on the right side of the road, another country on the left side. In comparison to this, in science, the word *law* should refer to a tentative working description of an observed behavior in the physical world, always subject to possible modification in the future.

The Object under Study Can Be Isolated or Controlled

In performing a scientific experiment, it's essential to isolate the device under test from undesired external influences, so these variations won't affect our measurements. We may need to control the temperature, the pressure, or the lighting; provide shielding from electromagnetic radiation; isolate the test setup from the vibration of the floor, and so on. Ideally, you want an experimental setup such that only one variable changes at any one time, strictly under your control.

A friend of mine was performing measurements of a very low-level electromagnetic field. He found that he kept getting unrepeatable results. After many months of frustrated attempts to get good data, he discovered that the central heating system in the building kept clicking on and off all day long, creating electromagnetic interference, which upset the measurements in his experimental setup. He was forced to perform all his experiments from then on between midnight and 6:00 a.m. inside a freezing cold building while the central heating system was turned off!

Social psychology tells us that no such thing as an individual in isolation from society exists. When people are isolated, this affects their behavior. People's behavior also changes if they know they are being observed.

Experiment Can Be Repeated in Order to Test for Validation

When we report our data taken from an experiment, ideally anyone in the world should be able to repeat our measurements and verify them by getting the same result. This repeatability requirement automatically rules out one-of-a-kind events.

If you reflect on your personal life history, you will see that you have experienced a long succession of important, life-changing events that would qualify as merely anecdotal, since they took place unexpectedly, not under a controlled environment, and there may not have been any unbiased witnesses present. The big earthshaking events in our lives, by their very nature, are once-in-a-lifetime experiences that can never be repeated: birth, first steps, being beaten by a school bully, first kiss, leaving home, loss of loved one, separation, crises, wartime, and so on.

> You cannot step into the same river twice.
> —Heraclitus

River is a metaphor for our experience of life as a transient, constantly changing force that challenges us as we struggle to not be swept away. A river can refresh me, guide me, transport me, make me lose control, overwhelm me, drown me, feed my crops. *Step into* is a metaphor for experiencing life. Heraclitus is saying that life is a never-ending succession of challenges and opportunities that never repeat. The nonrepeating quality of life is highlighted here. Heraclitus has succeeded in illustrating this in a very compact, visual way. As you reflect on all the years you've lived, you will probably acknowledge that this is true for you.

Objective Results Are Required

The results of an experiment should be reported in such a way that they are totally independent of who you, the experimenter, are. Your subjective self, personal history, characteristics, and beliefs should not influence the reported results.

An article appeared in a New York newspaper: some youths had robbed a small grocery store and then ran away with the money. The police arrived and gave chase. The police yelled to stop, but the youths kept on running. As the youths jumped over a fence, a policeman shot one of them in the back. The youth jumped in the air and fell backward, yelling at the top of his lungs, "Jesus Christ!"

A reporter appeared later to interview the people involved. One of the policemen declared, "This kid was an animal. Can you imagine? He blasphemed right at the moment of his death!"

The reporter then noticed a woman crying nearby. It was the dead youth's mother. He went over and interviewed her. She exclaimed, crying loudly, "My Johnny, he was a good boy! He died with a prayer on his lips!"

Facts are not enough. Data is not the last word. What is really important is the interpretation of the data.

Beauty

It is interesting to note that beauty can be one of the elements that draws many of us into the field of science. However, science is incapable of measuring beauty. You cannot quantify beauty for one thing, and for another, the experience of beauty is dynamic and subjective; different people will have different responses when exposed to the exact same experience.

We have already seen how science can be indebted to beauty. At the same time, however, science is unable to measure beauty. I love beauty, and I'm drawn to it. To access the full, deep, rich expressions of all forms of beauty, we are forced to include the natural world, all human art forms, plus the inner personal, one-of-a-kind beauty of people. We desperately need art and spirituality!

Morality

The history of science gives us many examples of the dedication of scientists of many nations to just causes. Yet science itself is amoral—morally neutral as to its applications. This is not a reflection on the practitioners of science; rather, it points out that scientists must go elsewhere to resolve issues of morality in the applications of science. The more powerful the tool, the more we need a moral use of it. Issues of morality have been dealt with through religion, philosophy, and popular values for millennia.

No one can question that science is constantly opening new worlds for us, new panoramas for us to pursue. Science has given us shelter from the weather; freedom from seasonal starvation; cures for diseases; and the spreading of knowledge through the incredible power of information storage, processing, and transmission. Science is certainly capable of producing morally good products and processes.

On the other hand, I am aware of hurtful things that are made possible by science (Barbour 1993; Goliszek 2003). I see the missile delivery systems used by both sides in a war. I see high technology that is used for efficient and minimally invasive surgery also being used for the trafficking of human organs. I see great advances in information retrieval that open a whole new world to us yet at the same time can be used for identity theft. We have observed cases in which scientists switch sides after a war is over, continuing to do the work they did before, just as if nothing at all had happened.

Science is a powerful tool, but a tool that doesn't tell me how to use it. We need to go outside science to determine the good or the evil of its application because science is essentially amoral.

> Science without conscience is the death of the soul.
> —Francois Rabelais (1494–1553)

> Why does this magnificent applied science which saves work and makes life easier bring us so little happiness? The simple answer runs: because we have not learned to make sensible use of it.
> —Albert Einstein, (1879–1955)
> Physicist

> No science is immune to the infection of politics and the corruption of power.
> —Jacob Bronowski

> Man's awesome scientific advances into the infinitude of space as well as the infinitude of sub—atomic particles seems most likely to lead to the destruction of our world unless we can make great advances in understanding

and dealing with interpersonal and intergroup tensions.

—Carl Rogers
Therapist

Significance or Meaning

I want you to picture a small boy—let's call him Timmy—who wants to buy his mom a present. Timmy has his allowance money in his pocket. He goes to the nearby discount store and sees a small bottle of perfume. Timmy checks in his pocket and sees he can afford the bottle. He takes the small bottle of perfume, goes to the counter, buys it, has it wrapped, and then goes home and gives to his mom it as a gift.

Suppose we had very accurately weighed the bottle, measured all its dimensions, drawn a graph of its appearance, and deduced its chemical composition both before and after Timmy chose it. We would've gotten the exact same results both times. No difference from before to after. Yet from the moment Timmy chose that bottle, the bottle was different; its significance changed. Science is incapable of measuring significance.

Significance has tremendous power to transform our lives. The fact that it cannot be detected by science does not mean it is not real!

Gift giving is a sacred art; it changes the giver, changes the recipient, and changes the relationship between the two forever.

Significance is of great value to human beings. It carries great weight in our hearts and our accumulated experience, yet science cannot detect it. Significance is essentially a spiritual issue. In issues of significance, we need to go beyond science.

We see the value that humanity gives to significance when we behold statues to fallen heroes, museum preservation of older paintings, historical newspaper headings, old photographs, recordings of famous speeches. For thousands of years, humans have had special rituals and places to bury their dead and visit them afterwards periodically, showing great reverence. We save a pressed flower, a wedding invitation, our old teddy bear, pictures of our grandparents, old love letters, baseball memorabilia, the Gutenberg Bible, the Declaration of Independence, the Dead Sea Scrolls, and so on.

A present given to us by a loved one carries the presence of the loved one in it. When a person dies, we treasure any object that belonged to him or her and can now put us in touch with him or her. It is irreplaceable; it has an infinite value to us.

When we use science as the only way of knowing, it can lead to us believe that we live in an uncaring universe, that life has no meaning. These things are not absent; it is our vision that selectively filters them out. Research by Aaron Antonovsky (Antonovsky, 1987), Viktor Frankl (Frankl, 1992), and Carl Jung (Mattoon, 1981, 232) has shown how essential meaning is to our mental health.

> Those who have a "why" to live, can bear with almost any "how."
>
> —Viktor E. Frankl
> Man's Search for Meaning

Personhood

I'm a psychiatrist, and I have studied human behavior for decades, but I still do not know why people do what they do. I have some understanding of human nature, but neither I nor my most experienced colleagues, with all the best scientific appraisals at our disposal,

can predict what a given person will think or
feel or do in the future.

—Gerald G. May
Psychiatrist

We get to know many people in our lives. We know people from work or school, our families, and other relatives. In a very real sense, every one of them is unique. You stop and think and focus on any one particular person—let's say that this is a friend you have known for a few years. As you think of this friend, you have obvious external information about him or her: age, physical appearance, education, marital status, hobbies, opinions about the world, and so on. Beyond these external descriptors of your friend, there is something unique, mysterious, dynamic, hard to define, and elusive that keeps shifting throughout time, sometimes radically, sometimes imperceptibly. This is the mystery of personhood!

Personhood is easier to experience than to define, yet personhood includes the living presence of that particular person, what defines him or her as being uniquely him- or herself. The experience of personhood in the other is mysterious, creative, subjective, partly hidden, always changing, and colorful. This encounter with the other's personhood is a deep part of life; it adds depth, texture, balance, challenge, and surprise to our existence.

A life without personhood would be a stilted, boring life consisting of ATMs, automatic teller machines that have predictable mechanical performance all the time. We cannot go to science to experience, categorize, and fully describe personhood in a meaningful way. Personhood in others and in ourselves is a dynamic mystery to be experienced with awe, not explained. Personhood belongs to the realm of spirituality.

The depth of our experience in relating to others is deeply involved in personhood. We need to look for this quality outside the limitations of science.

Presence

In the course of our daily lives, it is very easy to take the presence of others for granted. It is only when a transition occurs that we become acutely aware of its power and importance. The feeling of presence forces itself upon us when we attend a birth and see a baby emerging for the first time, a unique, mysterious someone who did not exist prior to that moment. We experience presence markedly when we fall in love; a new person is now at the center of our lives. Presence is also very acutely experienced during moments of separation: moving away or the breakup of a relationship. Another moment in which we have acute awareness of presence is at the death of a loved one. The loved one transitions from being tangibly present to us externally to being present to us only within our internal world.

When a baby goes through the terrifying process of being born, the baby's awareness of a loving presence welcoming him or her is essential at that moment, as it will also be all throughout his or her life development. Lack of a loving presence in a person's development has a marked impact on his or her growth; this absence is capable of bringing on many human maladies later on.

Presence cannot be measured by science since it is not quantitative, and it is subjective.

Viktor Frankl was a Jewish therapist who was imprisoned in a concentration camp for three years during World War II, forcibly separated from his wife, Tilly, who had been taken to another camp: "My mind still clung to the image of my wife. A thought crossed my mind: I didn't even know if she were still alive. I knew only one thing—which I have learned well by now: Love goes very far beyond the physical person of the beloved. It finds its deepest meaning in his spiritual being, his inner self. Whether he is actually present, whether or not he is still alive at all, ceases somehow to be of importance" (Frankl 1959). Our loved ones continue to have presence inside us even after they have died!

Our Private Inner World

As we go through everyday life, we have some experiences that can be observed by everybody around us. Likewise, we have experiences that only we have some awareness of. It is convenient to use the metaphors of *outer* (visible to myself and others) and *inner* (hidden from others and, in part, also hidden from myself) to distinguish between these two important worlds.

Our outer world refers to things we are involved in that other people can readily observe from the outside. The outer world is the obvious one: the world of cars, desks, meetings, conversations, sports, friendships, computers, production lines, and so on. Our inner world refers to experiences that only we can have some limited awareness of: memories of our entire, unique, idiosyncratic life histories; our constant energy flow of emotions; our flights of imagination; visualizations; creativity; our search for love and meaning. The inner world also includes our dark side: anger, resentments, prejudices, blind spots, frustrations at dead-end efforts, fears, destructive emotions, intuitions, insights, reflections, goals.

As we review human history, bringing it down to the personal details of the leaders who were in command, we can see how the inner life of one individual can have tremendous impact on others, both for good and for evil. Every one of us, to the extent that we have power over others, has the capacity to hurt him- or herself and others by us being unawares of this dark inner side. We all have a deep moral responsibility to know our inner worlds, including our dark sides.

Through many years of grueling engineering courses, I was taught only about the external world. No mention was ever made of the existence of anything else. We now spend a fortune looking for intelligent life millions of light-years away, yet we pay very little or no attention to our inner worlds.

We can't access our inner worlds using voltmeters, logic analyzers, computers, or imaging machines. Measuring mass, electrical charge, spatial coordinates, velocity, acceleration, pH—none of these tell us what is happening in our inner worlds. There is essential mystery residing in ourselves and in others. Since external physical measurements can't access the contents of our inner worlds, it's natural to ask what we can do to connect with our inner worlds. Time-honored tools used for self-knowledge include prayer and reflection, meditation, keeping a depth journal (see the chapter on spiritual practices), and cultivating quality close friendships. Close relationships can produce what is called reflected self-awareness: people who interact with us at a close level can act as virtual mirrors to give us brief glimpses of who we are. These necessary insights are always limited and contain the bias and limitations of the person doing the mirroring.

From birth through childhood, infancy, teenage years, young adult life, and old age, we never achieve full self-knowledge. The challenge of self-knowledge always leaves us with an awareness of the remaining mystery. Our important challenge of knowing ourselves never ends.

I realize that increasing my self-knowledge is really important because our inner worlds have deep and lasting impacts on our life journeys and on our interactions with others around us. As much as I love physical science, I feel a strong need to step beyond it in order to pursue self-knowledge using the other tools from the domain of spirituality that are available to me.

How Versus Why

Newton was very honest in stating that he could not explain why his theory of universal gravitation worked; all he knew was that it did. This is a classic example of being able to describe (explaining how) without having to postpone the results until the explanation (Why?) could be known. Physical science can describe how something happens without being held back by waiting for a deeper explanation. The temptation can be to go one step further and use science to make claims about why things are just the way they are. Science gives us the numbers we get from data; the explanation of why they are that way is not forced on us.

Love

Love is one more essential component of our ability to thrive in life that cannot be studied by science since it is mysterious, dynamic, and subjective. Love is not numerical and cannot be isolated.

"Basically, we seem to be embarrassed by the subject of love. There are a number of reasons for this state of affairs. One is the confusion between genuine love and romantic love…Another is our bias toward the rational, the tangible and the measurable in 'scientific medicine'…Since love is an intangible, incompletely measurable and suprarational (transcending reason) phenomenon, it has not lent itself to scientific analysis" (Peck 1978, 174).

"To be in love is to experience hundreds of small successive feelings that you never quite experienced in that way before, as if another half of life has been opened up to you for the first time: a frenzy of admiration, hope, doubt, possibility, fear, ecstasy, jealousy, hurt, and so on and so on…Love is submission, not decision. Love demands that you make a poetic surrender to an inexplicable power without counting the cost" (Brooks 2015, 170–2).

"In short, the essential ingredient of successful psychotherapy is love…Intensive psychotherapy in many ways is a process of reparenting…For the most part, mental illness [barring brain damage] is caused by an absence of or defect in the love that a particular child required from its particular parents for successful maturation and spiritual growth. (Peck 1978, 173 and 175).

> Someday, after mastering the winds, the waves, the tides and gravity, we shall harness for God the energies of love, and then, for a second time in the history of the world, man will have discovered fire.
>
> —Pierre Teilhard de Chardin

Reflections

I graduated from graduate school full of knowledge, eager to apply it outside in the real world. However, I kept hitting brick walls. I was married and raising two children, and I had to start from square one! The care and upkeep of personal relationships. Recognizing uniqueness and the influence and importance of past life history in another person. The total absence of control environments in the day-to-day interactions with other people. The total lack of numbers or instruments as a means of making a decision. My background gave me no guidelines as to how to make ethical decisions in my work. Nobody told me I had an inner world or emotions or a subjective self. My greatest challenge was in learning how to know and love others and myself.

I was forced to recalibrate my vision of the world by learning to accept ambiguous and sometimes even self-contradictory information.

For Further Reading

Artigas, Mariano. 2000. *The Mind of the Universe: Understanding Science and Religion.* West Conshohocken, PA: Templeton Foundation Press.

Barbour, Ian G. 1990. *Religion and Science: Historical and Contemporary Issues.* San Francisco: Harper One.

Smith, Huston. 1976. *Forgotten Truth: The Common Vision of the World's Religions.* New York: HarperCollins.

Maslow, Abraham H. 1966. *The Psychology of Science: A Reconnaissance.* Washington, DC: Henry Regnery Company.

Kuhn, Thomas S. 1970. *The Structure of Scientific Revolutions.* Chicago: University of Chicago Press.

Chapter 5
What Does It Mean to Be Human?

Preview

So far, we have done an overview of the issues of history, the use of language, and the foundational ways of approaching truth in both science and spirituality from a very broad perspective. We will now move on to consider things from a more individual, personal point of view. We now ask the question "Given that I now have a broad vision, how do I respond to these new insights at the level of my personal attitudes, actions, and goals?"

> Know thyself.
>
> —Ancient Greek aphorism

The Importance of Our Worldview

I had a very vivid experience some years ago when I was working in very sunny Arizona. Normally, when I got up every morning, I had a well-planned strategy for commuting to work. One day I got up as usual and realized that I was not going to my normal job location, but to a new contractor's location, which was much farther away than my office and that I was going to be late. I panicked! I ran out the door wearing my dark sunglasses in a rush to get to my early appointment. When I arrived at the contractor's offices, I entered a four-story building without a single window in it. All of a sudden, I realized that I had left my regular glasses back at home, and I was wearing my very dark sunglasses instead.

I spent an entire day inside a building with no windows to the outside world. I attended meetings, going from conference room to conference room all day long, transacting business with total strangers for the very first time. It was a horrible experience! Everybody looked ghoulish green. All the walls and furniture looked different shades of gray-green. Everything was covered with shadows and darkness, like walking from room to room in some catacombs. When I got back home I was able to put on my regular glasses again, and I experienced huge relief.

My sunglasses took on the role of affecting my experience of the world, a metaphor for my worldview. This experience made very tangible to me how our worldview colors/filters how we see the world around us. When we look out at the world, we are seeing it, interpreting it, valuing it, through the filter of our worldview. We're not aware of our worldview; it's only when it becomes limiting or destructive and we suffer a lot that we might be forced to begin questioning it.

For those of us trained and indoctrinated in science, our worldview closely follows the expectations, techniques, values, and insights of the scientific method. The scientific worldview is useful for solving practical technical problems of machine-like processes involving mass, space, and energy, but trying to apply this technique to all our personal issues can cause problems in our self-awareness, our relationships with others, and our overall philosophy of life.

Properties

In math, physics, chemistry, and biology we are used to the fact that, in order to study a new problem, we begin by identifying the properties of the object or process being studied. For example, in math, the operation of addition has a commutative property, which says that when we add two numbers, the order in which we add them does not matter. In other words, a + b = b + a.

Material objects possess mass whose motion is described by Newton's laws of force and motion. Chemical elements have properties given in the periodic table of the chemical elements: "Silicon is a chemical element with the symbol *Si* and atomic number 14. A hard and brittle crystalline solid with a blue-gray metallic luster, it is a tetravalent metalloid. It is a member of group 14 in the periodic table, along with carbon above it and germanium, tin, lead, and flerovium below. It is not very reactive, although more reactive than carbon, and has great chemical affinity for oxygen" (Wikipedia).

We can accomplish things in science only by obeying these properties. They are our gasoline, our driver's licenses, our passports that allow us to move forward. When we ignore these properties, we can hit a brick wall, ending up in frustration and failure.

In science, we typically follow this sequence when dealing with a new object for our research:

1. Get to know its properties.
2. Obey its properties.

The overarching theme that runs through all technology is that we may have some control over nature only if we obeying its properties; nothing else works.

We, as human beings, also have some properties. We can't move forward in the human domain without knowing and obeying our own human properties. Important human properties include our personal life development, our religious training and experiences, our ability to recognize our spiritual needs, our ability to communicate effectively with others, our balance in diverse forms of intelligences, our ability to satisfy our many needs, and our self-knowledge.

Human Needs (Maslow)

Psychologist Abraham Maslow was one of the founders of the school of humanistic psychology (Maslow 1968). His thinking was surprisingly original—most psychology before him had been concerned with the abnormal and the ill. He, instead, wanted to know what constituted positive mental health. Humanistic psychology gave rise to several different therapies, all guided by the idea that people possess the inner resources for growth and healing and that the point of therapy is to help remove obstacles to individuals' achieving this. Maslow spent considerable time studying what human beings need to survive and thrive. He came up with eight groups of human needs that are widely used to identify the essential components of human mental health.

Transient Needs for Coping (1–4)

1. Biological and physiological needs: air, food, drink, shelter, warmth, sex, sleep, et cetera
2. Safety needs: protection from the elements, security, order, law, limits, stability, et cetera
3. Social needs: belongingness and love, work group, family, affection, relationships, et cetera
4. Esteem needs: self-esteem, achievement, mastery, independence, status, dominance, prestige, managerial responsibility, et cetera

Needs for Growth (5–8)

5. Cognitive needs: knowledge, meaning, et cetera

6. Aesthetic needs: appreciation and search for beauty, balance, form, et cetera

7. Self-actualization needs: realizing personal potential, self-fulfillment, seeking personal growth and peak experiences. creativity, spontaneity

8. Transcendence needs: helping others to achieve self-actualization, compassion, empathy, agape

Self-actualizing people tend to focus on problems outside themselves, have a clear sense of what is true and what is phony, are spontaneous and creative, and are not bound too strictly by social conventions.

Peak experiences are profound moments of love, understanding, happiness, or rapture, when a person feels more whole, alive, self-sufficient and yet a part of the world and more aware of truth, justice, harmony, goodness, and so on. Self-actualizing people can have many such peak experiences.

Science is of great help to us in our being able to satisfy biological, physiological, safety, and some cognitive (knowledge) needs.

Spirituality can make it possible for us to satisfy our social, esteem, cognitive (knowledge and meaning), aesthetic, self-actualization, and transcendence needs.

Meeting Human Needs

Science is important for

- Biological needs
- Physiological needs
- Safety needs
- Cognitive (knowledge) needs

Spirituality is important for
- Social needs
- Esteem needs
- Cognitive (knowledge or meaning) needs
- Aesthetic needs
- Self-actualization needs
- Transcendence needs

We definitely need science to improve our quality of life and to give us more options to choose from, yet science is not enough. I need much more than science as my guide in life because of my human particularities.

Man does not live by bread alone.
—Jesus

Leading a Healthy Life

Aaron Antonovsky (1923–1994) was an Israeli medical sociologist who was very interested in identifying human traits and beliefs that were health producing, as opposed to behaviors that were disease producing. He carried out extensive research on women, including a group who had survived the concentration camps of the Second World War. To his surprise, he found that these Holocaust survivors had the capability of maintaining good health and leading good lives despite all they had gone through. He found that 29 percent of these women survivors had positive emotional health in spite of the ordeals they had gone through. He found out that they had three characteristics in common:

114

1. Meaningfulness: a belief that things in life are interesting and a source of satisfaction, that things are really worth it, and that there is good reason to care about what happens. (Spirituality tells us that all life is meaningful and that it has a positive transcendent purpose.)

2. Comprehensibility: a belief that things happen in an orderly and predictable fashion and a sense that you can understand events in your life and reasonably predict what will happen in the future. (Science and spirituality share in the central belief in the *mind of the universe*, which says the universe is not capricious but orderly and can be understood to some degree.)

3. Manageability: a belief that you have the skills or ability, the support, the help, or the resources necessary to take care of things, and that things are manageable and within your control. (Spirituality emphasizes positive thinking.)

According to Antonovsky, the first element, meaningfulness, is the most important. If a person believes there is no reason to persist and survive and confront challenges, if he or she has no sense of meaning, then he or she will have no motivation to comprehend and manage events. His essential argument is that health producing depends on experiencing a strong sense of coherence. His research demonstrated that the sense of coherence predicts positive health outcomes.

"There are data which show religiosity to be positively correlated with health...In other words, the experiences which one has when one has strong religious beliefs and engages in religious practices can lead to a strong 'Sense of Coherence'" (Antonovsky 1995).

Figure 12 Viktor Frankl

The Human Need for Meaning

Viktor Frankl was a physician and therapist living in Vienna during World War II. He was responsible for the so-called suicide pavilion, where he treated very large numbers of women who had suicidal tendencies. In 1942 Frankl, his wife, and his parents were deported to Nazi concentration camps. Ultimately, only Frankl and his sister Stella survived.

Liberated after three years in concentration camps, Frankl returned to Vienna, where he developed and lectured about his own approach to psychological healing. Frankl believed that people are primarily driven by a "striving to find meaning in one's life," and that it is this sense of meaning that enables people to overcome painful experiences. One of the most important contributions that spirituality makes to us is to offer us a life rich in meaning!

"Life is never made unbearable by circumstances, but only by lack of meaning and purpose...A positive spiritual life practice can provide us with a rich sense of meaning and purpose" (Frankel 1959).

Human Intelligences (Gardner)

The human mind has a rich, multidimensional quality to it that provides it with the ability to thrive in a bewildering variety of

116

environments. We possess a multiplicity of potential talents that are meant to complement and aid one other. Balance is achieved by acknowledging, valuing, and working on developing all our talents. When only one skill is highly developed and used all the time to the exclusion of the other parts, we can develop blind spots and become stuck, out of balance.

Howard Earl Gardner is an American developmental psychologist and professor of education at Harvard University who disagreed with the standard theory of one-dimensionally measuring intelligence via the intelligence quotient (IQ) test. Gardner developed a theory of multiple intelligences to provide a useful model for education (Gardner 1993, 552–3).

Here is a brief outline of Howard Gardner's multiple intelligences:

> 1. Verbal-linguistic intelligence (well-developed verbal skills and sensitivity to the sounds, meanings, and rhythms of words). This skill can allow us to gain insights by better interpreting and processing the meanings of both technical and spiritual writings.
>
> 2. Logical-mathematical intelligence (the ability to think conceptually and abstractly and the capacity to discern logical and numerical patterns). This skill allows us to use logic in solving problems and to think quantitatively.
>
> 3. Spatial-visual intelligence (the capacity to think in images and pictures, to visualize accurately and abstractly). This allows us to do technical work in spatial dimensions and to use our visual imaginations to establish a sense of place when praying or reading scripture. This can also be used when praying with icons, as is done in Eastern churches.

4. Bodily-kinesthetic intelligence (the ability to control one's body movements and to handle objects skillfully). Dance can provide a joyful form of worship.

5. Musical intelligence (the ability to produce and appreciate rhythm, pitch, and timbre). Music and singing can be integral parts of prayer.

6. Interpersonal intelligence (the capacity to detect and respond appropriately to the moods, motivations, and desires of others). This will help us be more loving by making us more acutely sensitive and responsive to the feelings of others.

7. Intrapersonal intelligence (the capacity to be self-aware and in tune with inner feelings, values, beliefs, and thinking processes). This skill is essential for dialoguing with our inner worlds and developing sensitivity to our emotions and those of others. Just as importantly, these skills will help us to grow in much-needed self-knowledge to guide our spiritual journeys.

8. Naturalist intelligence (the ability to recognize and categorize plants, animals, and other objects in nature). Spirituality in our century has to be sensitive to experiencing and taking care of nature as a source of wonder.

9. Existential intelligence (the sensitivity and capacity to tackle deep questions about human existence such as: What is the meaning of life? Why do we die? How did we get here?) These unescapable questions can provide an important starting point and motivation for our spiritual journeys.

An intensive science-only education can fine-tune our logical-mathematical and spatial-visual intelligences very heavily, possibly leaving our other intelligences neglected and underdeveloped. The task ahead for us is to work on filling in the gaps created by our formal education and our work culture.

A Sense of Worth by Association

Being active contributors to modern science and technology can puff us up by our association with these fields' enormous success and power. It's a heady trip to be able to participate in the success of such a powerful movement! The effect of this association can lead to an overvaluing of ourselves because of our technical knowledge, leading to our seeing people around us who are not technical as being somehow inferior. The resulting outcome can at times lead to unconscious arrogance. I once saw a man walking down the street wearing a T-shirt that read "As a matter of fact, I AM A ROCKET SCIENTIST!"

A feeling of being superior to others can deeply affect our relationships with other people. We will have a harder time getting close to people if we feel superior to them. Besides distancing us from nontechnical people, a feeling of superiority can have an even more pervasive negative effect: it can block us from being open to learning new, unfamiliar things that lie outside our comfort zones.

I grew up in Mexico at a time when there were large multitudes of destitute, illiterate people all around me. Many times, I felt humbled observing their obvious wisdom and versatility in handling very difficult problems of day-to-day survival while keeping their families lovingly together through very difficult times. I was humbled by these observations and learned to value the natural, unschooled intelligence of humans.

> The first step to knowledge is to know I am ignorant.
> —Socrates

119

It's hard to enter into a deeper understanding of spirituality if I feel I have already succeeded and I already know everything. To move on to expanding my mind first requires acknowledging the limitations of my present knowledge base. Keeping in mind Howard Gardner's multiple intelligences can make us aware of how many distinct skills beside ours it takes to keep the world meeting day-to-day challenges while moving forward. We can realize how limited our own expertise is in comparison to the total picture: playfulness, creativity, artistic expression, response to suffering, the maintenance of loving relations during trying times, and communication and practical problem-solving skills, among other things. We are one, and only one, part of a richly varied humanity.

> A specialist is a person who knows more and more about less and less until they know all about nothing.
> —William J. Mayo
> (Credited)

Keep in mind that no matter how competent and maybe even famous you may be in your work, this is not really who you are, not the totality of you. You have many other sides to your personality, some developed, some dormant. Your professional accomplishments will one day be outdated and cast aside, perhaps even laughed at. I knew a man who did wonderful work in the early stages of electronics technology, but when he wrote his résumé many years later, he had to be very sure to carefully omit any mention of what specific technology he had worked on because he would have been automatically dismissed as being hopelessly outdated, and no one would have talked to him, much less hired him!

It is important for our health and wholeness that we acknowledge and enjoy also being the broader us that is not defined by work. Who we are as individuals transcends our work titles. Overidentifying with our work roles can produce inauthentic, one-dimensional illusions, flat cardboard people. I am not a scientist, no matter how much I like the title and the prestige associated with it. I happen to work in a science-related field in which I have accumulated knowledge and experience in a focused, small specialty. *Ulrich's Periodicals Directory* (41st edition, 2003) has a listing of thousands of periodicals that are published every year. In addition to my own specialty, there are thousands of other specialties that in practical terms are totally outside my reach.

If I am a scientist for my work and I value the language and methods of science exceedingly and exclusively, I can begin to think that these are so good that any other problem-solving methods are inferior and not necessary.

Work comes and goes; it changes as technology, the economy, and trends change. People who overidentify with their work roles can be devastated when they lose their jobs, when their families fall apart, or when they retire.

The Many-Faceted Quality of Reality

There is an ancient spiritual teaching story that has been passed among several religious traditions. The story tells us that at one time, there were six blind men living in a village. An elephant came to their village for the first time, and the six men went out to meet it. One blind man touched the tail and said, "An elephant is just like a snake—long and skinny." The second blind man touched the elephant's ear and said, "An elephant is like a giant lily pad—big and flat and smooth." The third blind man touched a leg and said, "An elephant is like a coconut tree—a tall pole going up into the air." The fourth blind man touched the stomach, and he said, "An elephant is like a great ball—big and round." The fifth blind man touched the elephant's mouth and said, "An elephant is a wet fruit opened up." The sixth blind man touched the elephant's tusk and said, "An elephant is like a long, curved pole."

This story points out visually that a part of reality cannot necessarily be generalized to cover all that exists. We need to cultivate humility and openness in our knowing.

We may be seeing the beginnings of the reintegration of our culture, a new possibility of the unity of consciousness. If so, it will not be on the basis of any new orthodoxy, either religious or scientific. Such a new integration will be based on the rejection of all univocal understandings of reality, of all identifications of one conception of reality with reality itself. It will recognize the multiplicity of the human spirit, and the necessity to translate constantly between different scientific and imaginative vocabularies. It will recognize the human proclivity to fall comfortably into some single literal interpretation of the world and therefore the necessity to be continuously open to the birth in a new heaven and a new earth (Bellah 1970).

Reality is multilayered or stratified, each layer demanding to be investigated and represented in different ways. An explanation that works well at one level doesn't necessarily work at another level. Our human knowing never takes in the whole elephant. It is not wise to claim we have the only truth and all others need to reconcile their views with ours. Science and religion each give us only part of the truth. An open, continuing dialogue and collaboration is needed among all human disciplines. Spirituality is multidimensional; it can be communicated via scholarly work, social activism, music, sculpture, painting, dance, cooking, gardening, closeness, presence, touch...

Spiritual Development (Fowler)

James W. Fowler, along with his associate Lawrence Kohlberg and his contemporaries Carol Gilligan and Daniel J.

Levinson, is widely regarded as a seminal figure in the field of developmental psychology (Fowler 1981).

Fowler was interested in studying and describing typical patterns in people's spirituality as they go through life. He did a study of people at different ages and different stages of development. He came up with a theory that attempts to show how our spirituality commonly goes through some six well-defined stages of growth. Not everybody agrees with this schema, but it serves to give us a starting place for reflection.

Here is a very brief description of the stages of spiritual growth proposed by Fowler:

- Stage 1 (ages 3 to 7): Religion is accepted without question through experiences, stories, images, and the people one comes in contact with.

- Stage 2: (school-age children): Metaphors and symbolic language used in stories are often taken literally.

- Stage 3: (early teens) Characterized by conformity to religious authority and the development of a personal identity. Any conflicts with one's beliefs are ignored at this stage because of the need to belong to our peer group.

- Stage 4: (usually midtwenties to late thirties) a stage of angst and struggle. The individual takes personal responsibility for his or her beliefs and feelings. As one is able to reflect on one's own beliefs, there is an openness to a new complexity of faith, but this also increases the awareness of conflicts in one's beliefs.

- Stage 5: (midlife crisis) The individual resolves conflicts from previous stages by a complex understanding of a multidimensional, interdependent "truth" that cannot be explained by any particular statement.

- Stage 6: The individual treats any person with compassion as he or she views people as from a universal community who should be treated with universal principles of love and justice. .

Imbalance

Many of us follow a growth pattern in which we grow up initially under the spheres of influence of our parents, schools, churches, and neighborhood friends, after which point we leave home to go to college. Our college experience can be a totally secular one, separate from our family of origin, our childhood place of worship, and our close friends from home.

In a technical college, our courses claim to give us tools for sensing, processing, and making conclusions about physical reality only, all of these being predominantly practical, technical, and secular. Very little, if any, attention is given to "soft-edge" human issues. We, in turn, can unconsciously believe that we have been given a broad picture of all of reality by our schools.

When we move on to enter our work world, we achieve our maturity by daily use of purely secular methods. The net effect of all this is that we can have two people, not one, inside us:

1. An adult whose development in science is that of a mature, college-trained grownup.

2. A person whose religious development, if any, stopped in his or her childhood or teenage years yet who today faces spiritual challenges that require an adult understanding of spirituality.

Our understanding of our professions and our understanding of religion can be at two completely different age levels. When we observe our professional secular level of development and then compare it to our religious mind-sets, our religious mind-sets can seem to us to be childlike because, in actuality, they can be. If this is the case, we need to move on beyond the level of a child in our religious awareness by committing to doing some adult-level studying of our faith of choice.

"Among all my patients in the second half of life...There's not been one whose problem in the last resort was not that of finding a religious outlook on life...And none of them had really been healed without regaining his religious outlook" (Jung et al 1964).

This does not mean we should automatically reject our parents' spiritual traditions or struggle to invent a new religion! If our upbringing gave us no faith foundation whatsoever and now we face adult issues of life (search for meaning, need for deep relationships with others, etc.), we need to seek spiritual foundations in response to our newly developed awareness. We need to reevaluate our prior beliefs by processing our adult lived experience while remaining open to what might develop in this search.

My **Image of God**

In his book *Your God is Too Small*, Episcopal priest J. B. Phillips talks about some common misconceptions about God that can limit people's growth (Phillips 1952). Here are just a few of them:

- God-in-a-Box

  Some religious institutions appear to be saying "You will jump through one particular hoop or sign on our particular dotted line so that we will introduce you to God. But if not, then there is no God for you."

- Resident Policeman

  God is identified with a still, small voice that makes us feel guilty and unhappy before or during any wrongdoing.

125

- Parental Hangover

Many psychologists believe that the trend of the whole of a person's life is strongly affected, but not totally defined, by his or her attitude in early years toward his or her parents. The early conception of God is almost invariably affected by the child's experience of their parents.

> Call no man Father.
> —Jesus

It can be an act of extreme frustration to feel compelled to mimic the spiritual styles of our parents, since spirituality is influenced markedly by our inborn temperaments. An extrovert will have a markedly different spirituality than an introvert. A person guided by intuition will have a markedly different spirituality than someone guided by use of his or her senses. Don't blindly imitate the spiritual style of another person or hero, no matter how highly you may think of them. Get to know yourself, and then be yourself.

- Grand Old Man

When some Sunday school children were asked what God was like, they said, "God is a very old gentleman living in heaven."

- Absolute Perfection

Some people believe that since God is perfection, the best way of serving God is to set one-hundred-percent-perfection standards to their performance.

- Managing Director

This belief sees God as being responsible for the terrifying vastness of the universe, and therefore God cannot possibly be interested in the lives of the minute specks of consciousness that exist on this insignificant planet (Phillips 1952).

Most of us had some exposure, intentional or accidental, to the idea of God when we were still very young. We took in and internalized this as children, with our limited experience, vocabulary, and capacity to interpret this image. We might have a painful experience or one involving guilt and accusation. We might observe a grownup being severe, judgmental, and unbending in the name of God. We might experience one of our parents being violent or manipulative, controlling. We might form part of our image of God based on first incidents of a small child, and these images will just not do for our adult life.

At some point, our child's image can turn out to be hurtful or limiting to us unless we reevaluate it. We need to reprocess our child's image of God and integrate it with our mature life experience. Our image of God will always be tentative and open to change as our lives unfold, and we grow in our capacity to interpret life events.

"When we are children our parents are godlike figures to our child's eye, and the way they do things seems the way they must be done throughout the universe. Our first (and sadly, often our only) notion of God's nature is a simple extrapolation of our parents' natures" (Peck 1978, 190).

Growth Rings

Some time ago, I was admiring a slab of wood from a beautiful old tree. The wood grain was so rugged and beautiful! This gave me an insight into how this pattern could function as a metaphor/analog/model for human growth. When we look at a tree, we see only its bark, its exterior; we are unaware of its inner structure in the form of rings. This is similar to when we meet a

person and can't see his or her past history. The outside bark of the tree is like the exterior appearance we present to others in the outer world. As the tree grows, every year it forms a new growth ring. Rings are added concentrically starting from the center and moving out. Every ring depends on the previous rings, all the way back to ring number one at the center. The inner rings represent our years of lived experience and the indelible mark they have left on our persons. I can never get rid of any ring since all the rings are

Figure 13 Growth rings in tree trunk

permanently interconnected. We humans are like that. We never outgrow or abandon our previous years of experience, our years of development, our previous "rings." I have a host of people inside me: a fifty-year-old, a forty-year-old, a thirty-year-old, a rebellious teenager, a scared little boy, a crying baby.

The outside ring, our present reality, is solidly attached to every one of our previous experiences and our processing of them as we could at that age level.

In other words: you are not one person only, but a complex group of people with different experiences, languages, and perceptions appropriate to their separate individual ages.

Figure 14 Russian nesting dolls

This reality is expressed very tangibly by Russian nesting dolls. On the visible outside is an adult. If I open it up, I see that there is a younger adult inside, then a younger person inside, then a teenager, then a child...all the way back to a newborn baby. If it is true that I react to life as a multiple group of persons of different life experiences and capacities, then any illusion I might have of being 100 percent rational at all times is just that—an illusion. I need to acknowledge the prerational parts of me, but this is hard for someone whose whole education was exclusively rational to do.

Knots

Figure 15 Knot in the wood

In looking at a weathered wooden bench, I noticed that in the wood, there were many hard, dark knots, a permanent part of the wood. Knots behave quite differently from the rest of the wood. Knots are extremely hard! Knots can break a saw, or they can fall off and weaken the wooden structure.

Our lives are also like this, we have painful past experiences, hurtful knots, indelibly encased into our growth rings. Knots happen, and we can't deny or remove them; they are permanent parts of us. We have to live with every one of our knots!

We can reexperience our knots when something in the present (a trigger) reminds us of the original experience that created the knot within us in the past. This trigger can be any of a large set of situations: a smell, a sight, a sound, a setting, a person.

It is very important to be aware of our trigger events. For one thing, it can help us to accept our apparently irrational behavior when it occurs. We also gain important insight into what painful incidents we have in our pasts.

Painful events in our pasts call out for healing from us. By journaling, talking, or sharing with close friends, we can bring some healing to our hurtful past experiences. Healing does not mean that the problem disappears; it means that we grapple with it and come to a point of acceptance. An unhealed hurt can overpower us. A healed hurt becomes a part of our traveling baggage, needing our patience and compassion. Conscious suffering from our knots can lead to compassion for others and for ourselves.

PTSD

Persons who have experienced traumatic events in their lives can develop what is called post-traumatic stress disorder (PTSD) (Matsakis 1992).

Traumatic events can be mundane (a dog biting me, a kid friend punching me, kids rejecting me on the playground, feeling inadequate with girls at a party) or life-shattering (violence in the home, the death of a close loved one, being beaten up, a lethal car crash, observing or participating in war violence, experiencing toxic shame).

Our minds deal with overwhelming events by shutting them off from our awareness "just for now" and dumping them into our unconscious ("knots in the inner layers"), to be dealt with someday later when we are stronger.

Trigger Events

A trigger event happens when I feel jettisoned out of my control, back into a hurtful past experience by an association in the present. (One of my "knots" becomes activated as if I were reexperiencing the original event right now.)

A trigger event can consist of a smell, a sound, a voice, music, a person, or an environment or situation similar to one in the past. Trigger events can bring on panic attacks grief, loss, fear, terror, anger, shame, revulsion, stomach upset, headaches, dizziness, unexplainable feelings not related to your present environment, and distortions in your world view.

I am not my outer bark; I am not my outermost ring. I am a sometimes-conflicting composite of all my layers and their knots, a village of many people of different ages, languages, and levels of development. I need to be alert and sensitive to the enduring presence of my past.

I can grow in self-awareness of my personal history by conversing with people who have been present throughout my life history. Journaling and reflecting will help me process these experiences.

Hurts from the past are like steer manure: when ignored, they sit giving off an awful smell. On the other hand, when attended to, they can be used to fertilize the growth of new flowers. When I take time to process my hurts from the past, I can grow to be a more open, experienced, and compassionate human being.

Hurtful experiences in the past never go totally away, they can overpower me in the present. When a trigger event happens, I need to be aware that this is happening and then create a sheltered, safe, loving environment for myself at that time.

> They that ignore the past are doomed to repeat it!
> —George Santayana

> Modern man does not believe that he has an unconscious. Little does he realize that his unconscious has him!
> —Carl Jung

Reflections

It came as a shock to me when I first realized I was looking at life through a narrow selective filter! In those days, when I walked into an electronic lab, I knew so much about all the equipment there but much less about myself, my coworkers, and my family. I became angry and resolved to change this situation. Life is just too precious to be undervalued in any way.

Some years ago, I did a life review in which I worked to discover my core values. I found these core values to be love; transcendence; beauty; meaning; and connectedness to God, the universe, and other people. I found gaps in my education, and I resolved to fill in these gaps gradually via reading, taking courses, and interacting with people from backgrounds different from my own. I set a long-term goal of developing a life vision that would open me up and propel me forward while keeping my sense of wonder alive. My life has become richer and more colorful. I am glad I took this journey!

I made four resolutions that I follow to the best of my abilities:

- I will strive to say no to pessimistic machinelike views of people and the universe.

- I will strive to learn to live with uncertainty, avoiding premature closure as a means of gaining security.

- I will strive to stay open to listening to and valuing other voices.

- I will work on cultivating an attitude of deep gratitude at all times. All is gift!

Needs

- Describe briefly what your technical education told you it means to be human. Compare this to what you have learned from your personal life experience.
- Describe briefly the worldview given to you by your technical education. What are its positives and negatives?
- Review Maslow's human needs one by one. Are there any needs in your personal life that require some more attention on your part today?
- Reflect on what a huge spectrum of talents other than the technical ones it takes to work in a complex society while maintaining deep loving relationships, making important life choices, and raising a family.

Your Personal History

- Spend time reviewing your unique life history. Make a list of some of the key events in your life, both positive and negative, that have had the deepest impact on you up till now.
- Describe your exposure, both formal and informal, to religious teachings throughout your life.
- How old were you the last time you were exposed to religious teachings? How does this age compare with your present professional and chronological ages?
- Do Fowler's stages of spiritual development give you any useful insights into your faith journey?
- Describe some of the positive and negative aspects of the religion you were taught.

– List some personal images (models) you have of God. Review these and, if needed, update them to match your accumulated life experience.

Your Hurts

– Review your life story, specifically looking for hurtful events—your knots.

– Are you aware of any trigger events affecting you?

– Discern how your painful knots have affected your life in the past and affect it in the present.

– Resolve to work on self-knowledge so as to increase your compassion for yourself and for others while giving you a glimpse into the mystery of being human.

Chapter 6
Our Emotions: Friends or Foes?

My Personal History

Recently, I had a very interesting experience. I had an upset stomach, and I went to look for my antacid tablets in the medicine cabinet. When I reached for the container, I was surprised to see that its labels had all faded and they were crumbling, practically falling off. The bottle of antacids had expired more than a year ago! I used to routinely depend on antacids to keep me going, but now, with my awareness of my emotions, I found out that I do not need antacids to solve my problems. I had learned to acknowledge my emotions instead of trying to counter them after the fact with medication. Since emotions are experienced in the body as well as in the mind, emotions that are not acknowledged can result in psychosomatic symptoms: that is, body maladies that seem to have no physical cause.

My technical education consisted of several thousand hours of intense study. During this entire educational process, I never once heard anyone say the words *emotion* or *feelings*. As I struggled day by day with my studies, I felt a strange tugging and pulling inside me: energies churning, propelling me forward, holding me back, turning me around, lifting me up, flattening me to the ground, almost as if a separate being or force were inside me. In my relations with people around me, I realized I disliked some people while favoring others. I trusted some while not trusting others. I had no idea that these invisible yet very tangible energies were feelings, that they had names, that they could become my intimate friends, that they were there to give me guidance and insights, to energize me, and to move me in the right direction.

At that time, my education was illuminating a path to allow me to see with the light of analytical reasoning. Simultaneously, outside that beam of light was a darkness that had not been acknowledged: my emotional human side. A long-term blind spot was unwittingly being created for me. Even today, I still struggle to extend that beam of light to be able to include the richness that is to be found waiting for me outside it.

Our world has fostered the stereotype of the detached scientist for an extremely long time. Anyone who has worked in a technical environment is aware of the wide gamut of emotions that are routinely experienced there. Reading the life stories of famous scientists brings to light how much of a role their emotions, intuitions, rivalries, likes and dislikes, personal qualities, and imaginations had to play, not only in their personal lives, but also in their accomplishments.

I desperately wanted to grow as a human being. I wanted to be able to take in the beauty and the greatness of spirituality, while also establishing deeper levels of human relatedness. I resolved to sensitize myself to what it means to have feelings, how to value them and use them for self-knowledge, to contact my subconscious, to grow in empathy for others, and to participate more fully in life.

> Self-knowledge decreases control from outside the person and increases control from within the person.
>
> —Abraham Maslow

Rationalism as a Beam of Light

Rationalism is a worldview in which the path to the truth is believed to be purely intellectual and deductive, with no attention given to physical senses, intuition, inspiration, emotions, or past life experience (Oatley and Jenkins 1996).

The Western world has a long tradition of emphasizing the use of reason to arrive at the truth. This exclusive emphasis on reason, which permeates our technical education in its totality, simultaneously reinforces in us an undervaluing and mistrust of human emotions.

Emotions are not simple. They can overlap; are messy; and can be hard to define, break down, or analyze. Emotions are not fully under our control. In spite of all this, they are an essential part of our lives. We cannot decide to be separated from our emotions. They will follow us wherever we go; they are an important property of what it means to be human. People who attempt to ignore their emotions can wind up being in bondage to their power, whereas working with our emotions can help us to move forward more effectively in our life choices.

When we act as pure rationalists, our self-awareness is totally limited to our fact-based reasoning. Rationalism asks us to ignore our inspirations, our intuitions, our imaginations, our personal past histories, our feelings, our values, and our body sensations. Our hard-earned experience, which comes from having lived life, is an important factor in decision making, yet we may not always be able to verbalize it. Life does not send us exclusively problems that are well-defined, with complete and unambiguous data.

Years of training to respond to reason exclusively does not create a purely rational person. It can produce a person at great conflict with his or her emotions. (Which never went away!)

In the 1960s psychologist B.F. Skinner founded the school of behaviorist psychology (Oatley and Jenkins 1996), which stated that only behavior that could be seen objectively, from the outside, could be studied with scientific accuracy. Since emotions could not be observed or measured externally, they in effect were ignored in modeling human behavior. The computer, with its handling of hard data exclusively, became the day-to-day working model for the human mind.

A computer offers a good model or metaphor for a purely rationalist operation:

Hard data in >> Orderly processing >> Hard data out.

Jean Piaget (1896–1980) (Piaget 1964) was a famous developmental psychologist, who carried out very extensive long-term observations of how children develop. Piaget concluded that a child does not reach the use of reason until he or she is about seven years old. An obvious conclusion of Piaget's result is that critical issues of development during the first seven years of a child's life take place exclusively relying on the child's emotional and internal resources plus the child's support and guidance from his or her caretakers. If we accomplished all this essential development without full use of reason, we should be open to learning to include, value, and trust our emotions now that we are adults.

If you observe children for a while, it will quickly become obvious to you that children exhibit the exact opposite of detachment! Children are bursting with intensely passionate attachments: constant motion; constant searching; constant curiosity; a sense of wonder and awe; taking things apart; seeking to be touched; playfully skipping instead of walking; needing to be held; doggedly clinging to favorite toys and objects; seeking friendships; passionate to move ahead, to learn new things, to go beyond the boundaries of their world. A child not driven by all these passions would never survive in the real world because of the immense amount of material that they need to experience, assimilate, and process.

Accepting the fact that emotions cannot be measured on the outside yet are very important to us, we realize that we are forced to use metaphors to talk about them.

- Including both mystery and metaphor in our self-awareness will empower us to live life more fully.

Including mystery can feel very uncomfortable for someone trained in purely analytical reasoning. We somehow have been led to expect that every problem can be stated clearly and has a well-defined statement and solution. An important transition is taking place here. One central issue in our relationship with our emotions is trust. We need to gradually develop a sense of trust in our feelings and in the whole idea of accepting mystery. Without accepting mystery, we will never be able to move forward on our spiritual journeys.

- Heart is a metaphor for that part of us that can process feelings, empathy, values, loving relationships, compassion, creativity, intuition, moral values, life calling, beauty, art, spirituality, and body sensations.

The emphasis on the use of reason as a means of finding the truth has been with us since at least the classical Greek age. Reason is a beautiful tool that has given us amazing insights and technical progress over the centuries. Yet like all tools, it has limited applicability. I recently purchased a fantastic new software program that has dozens of powerful features, but I cannot use it to dig up weeds or fix the toilet or mend a broken relationship, no matter how attractive a product it is.

Overidentification with reason leads to our being out of touch with our feelings. We need to know when to apply reason and when to use it as only one part of a larger, richer set of tools. Reason and emotions are complementary essentials for our wholeness and well-being.

I like to think of myself as a recovering rationalist. As such, I have, at different times, held one of the three following attitudes toward the use of reason. This breakdown treats rationalism as occurring at one of three different levels, depending on how seriously it is taken as an exclusive judge of all truth. All levels can involve degrees of denial, or selective attention, a blocking of some aspects of reality.

Here are three practical levels of rationalist beliefs that I have personally experienced during my life. See if you can identify with any of these:

1. If something couldn't be proven by reason, I was not interested at all.

I presently don't like this position for two reasons: first of all, brushing things aside without considering them can create a blind spot for us, and we can wind up living inside a closed, comfortable box. Science can move ahead only by stretching the sides of the box of our present beliefs. Second, I can think of many deep, life-changing experiences I've lived through that cannot be proven by reason yet are an unescapable part of my life history. We invariably are confronted with nonnumerical, incomplete, and muddled information, obtained under conditions that are out of our control, in which the variables are not isolated from their environment.

2. If something couldn't be proven by reason, I couldn't tell if it was true or false; I was incapable of deciding.

This, my past position, clearly could lead me to paralysis. Life demands a response from us many times, regardless of whether the problem at hand has clear data and clear choices and is well-defined or not.

3. If something couldn't be proven by reason, I knew for sure that it was false.

When doing original research, the early stages of grappling with the problem are typically ill defined and nonverbal. That is, we have a felt assurance that we are on the right track, yet we cannot verbalize the solution from beginning to end. Not having a complete grasp of the problem or not having a complete overview is no excuse for us to stop the process. Creativity demands that we work in a preverbal stage before we can clean things up and then refine our understanding of the problem. One of my math professors used to say "Elegance is a form of embalming!"

I am now aware that when reason is not enough, we still have many other ways at our disposal to work toward getting at the truth. As wonderful a tool as reason is, we need to balance it with our emotions, intuitions, visualizations, inner voices, and insights from our own and others' past life experiences.

- Knowledge can be expressed and defended with reason, but wisdom is what we know is true yet just can't seem to verbalize its justification.

> Life is not a problem to be solved, but a mystery to be lived.
> —Soren Kierkegaard

> The heart has reasons which reason knows not of.
> —Blaise Pascal

> That which is really true can be seen only with the heart.
> —Antoine de Saint Exupery

I love the use of reason! I love its elegance and clean, crisp boundaries! Ever since I was a child, I have read about philosophy and the use of reason by great scientists and thinkers. I would never want to let go of this. Because of my training in science, whenever possible, I seek to define the problem at hand clearly, break it into its separate parts, analyze the parts individually, and then put them all together. This method has served me well over the years in my technical work. There are important times, however, when it becomes necessary to include other of our problem-solving faculties. Not all human problems can be well defined. In life, we are confronted with many problems that cannot be reduced to simple logical statements. We need to go beyond the use of strict reason when dealing with problems that are ill defined, murky, fuzzy, sometimes self-contradictory, hiding inside of one of our blind spots, when some type of a leap other than straight reason is required of us.

With age and lived experience comes some wisdom. We need to be open to listening to the many voices of our personal experience dwelling within us, even though we might not be able to verbalize how our experience gave us those results or be able to justify them by reason alone.

Our imaginations will allow us to visualize solutions to the problem at hand without having yet gone through a formal process of reasoning.

Our intuitions can suggest some possible solutions to try out. We need to allow our creative sides to give us insights that appear spontaneously before we can even verbalize them. These insights come from deep within us, our view of reality, and our relations to other people.

When struggling with self-knowledge or with our relations to other people, we always need to assign an important value to all the emotions involved. We need to be sensitive to emotions within ourselves: what they're telling us about our values, our needs, our prejudices, our perceptions. We need to be empathetic to the other person's emotions as well so as to include the person as a unique individual, not just as an object. Because of the complexity of our emotional makeup, it takes patience, openness, and trial-and-error to discern what is behind emotional expressions, both in ourselves and in the person we are relating to.

To enrich our lives, we can complement our former exclusively analytical approach with a patient, open-ended, empathetic, trial-and-error method. A lifelong creative dialogue between our rational and our emotional sides is very important.

Properties of the Emotions

Emotions are intense, highly personal internal feelings, which seem to have a life of their own and which can be very difficult to describe to others (Oatley and Jenkins 1996; Goleman 1995, 34, 39, 43, 46, 47, 51–4, and 291; McKay, Rogers, and McKay 1989).

Emotions are fast, instantaneous, spontaneous, not totally under our control. They are first responders that seek to prod us into action. No reflection is involved at this level; we can learn to ignore emotions, but we can never shut them off. We experience emotions 24/7, even when asleep.

"The emotional mind is far quicker than the rational mind, springing into action without pausing even a moment to consider what it is doing…Actions that spring from the emotional mind carry a particularly strong sense of certainty…Emotions mobilize us to respond to urgent events without wasting time pondering whether to react or how to respond…The full heat of emotion is very brief, lasting just seconds. We cannot choose emotions which we want to have" (Goleman 1995, 34, 39, 43, 46, 47, 51–4, and 291).

Emotions are experienced in the body, not just in the mind. Some common signs of suppressed feelings can be muscle tension; headache; indigestion; shaking; clammy hands; blurred vision; physical pain with no medical cause; depression; nausea; boredom; agitation or anxiety; dizziness; and the involuntary urge to overeat, overspend, overwork, abuse alcohol or drugs, or hurt yourself (Matsakis 1992).

In physical science, we are always trying to express our variables in universal and nonoverlapping terms (i.e., voltage, current, time, distance, and the like). Emotions are more complicated than that. They are hard to define; they can overlap, and their definitions and importance can vary from culture to culture.

One common situation in which we can see overlapping emotions is in our relationships with our parents. We can feel love and admiration toward a parent and yet at the same time feel disappointments and misgivings about him or her. Feeling both positive and negative emotions toward a person makes our relationship with them complex and many times frustrating. A vivid example of overlapping emotions occurs when we reflect on all the emotions that Shakespeare's Othello must feel as he is about to strangle his beloved wife Desdemona.

A List of Some Common Emotions

Having worked in electronics and mathematics over many years, my first instinct is to define emotions and then make an exhaustive, orderly list of them: clearly define what you're talking about, and break it down into parts.

As I surveyed the different lists of emotions proposed by different authors and compared them to my own personal life experiences, I realized that something was wrong. We cannot set a bound to the number of emotions, their gradations, and their overlaps. Think about your own experience: think of two musical pieces that you like. Even though you use the word *like* in both cases, the experience of hearing the first musical pieces is not the same as that of hearing the second musical piece. You say "like" or "don't like" in conversation, and the other person will shake his or her head, agreeing with you. But what he or she calls "like" and what you call "like" are not necessarily the same experience.

- The range of human experiences and our emotional responses to them are unbounded; they far outstrip the language we use to express them. We need all the arts to help us express a wider range of our lived experiences than those that can be expressed by reason alone.

For practical purposes, I find it helpful to show a list of emotions, while realizing that this does not exhaust all that can happen. It's useful to have both a long and a short list. The long list gives me a reference to refer back to. The short list is something I can carry around in my memory to ask myself what I am feeling right now or what might this other person be feeling right now.

Our family cultures and our gender can influence what emotions are acceptable to acknowledge and which ones are forbidden. Some families use anger to cover almost all emotions, while other families discourage expressions of anger. Some emotions like jealousy or envy can be seen as "feminine" and may not be readily acknowledged by men.

When an emotion is too threatening or shameful to us, we sometimes cover it up with the smokescreen of anger (McKay, Rogers, and McKay 1989).

A useful short list of emotions consists of anger, sadness, joy, and fear. A longer list with some expansions follows (Goleman 1995, 289; Bradberry and Greaves 2003, 95):

- Anger: a response to a perceived injustice or threat to your body, your property, your freedom to act, or your

146

self-esteem. Fury; outrage; resentment; wrath; exasperation; indignation; vexation; acrimony; animosity; annoyance; irritability; hostility; and, perhaps at the extreme, pathological hatred and violence.

- Sadness: a response to loss, absence, separation, or powerlessness. Grief; sorrow; cheerlessness; gloom; melancholy; self-pity; loneliness; dejection; despair; and when pathological, severe depression.

- Fear: a response or instinctive sensation that something bad is going to occur. Anxiety; apprehension; nervousness; concern; consternation; misgiving; awareness; qualm; edginess; self-protection; a perceived threat to me; dread; fright; terror; and as a psychopathology, phobia and panic.

- Joy: happiness; enjoyment; relief; contentment; bliss; delight; amusement; pride; sensual pleasure; thrill; rapture; gratification; satisfaction; euphoria; whimsy; ecstasy; and at the far edge, mania and self-satisfaction.

- Love: experiencing acceptance, friendliness, trust, kindness, affinity, devotion, peacefulness, adoration, infatuation, agape.

- Surprise: a response to a sudden or unexpected event. Shock, astonishment, amazement, wonder, suddenness.

- Disgust: contempt, distain, scorn, abhorrence, aversion, distaste, revulsion.

- Shame: a sense that I have not just done something bad, but that I myself am bad, unacceptable. Guilt, embarrassment, chagrin, remorse, humiliation, regret, mortification, and contrition.

Empathy

One of the most urgently needed qualities in our broken world today is empathy. Empathy is the ability to accept and feel similar emotions to what another person is feeling, to put ourselves in his or her shoes.

If we are talking with a teenager who has just been rejected in love, instead of brushing off his or her feelings, we need to use our memory and imagination to return to that particular mind-set we had at that age—our vulnerability, our fears, our need for acceptance—and then, from this mind-set, feel what that teenager might be feeling now in the present.

- Empathy requires my being able to know my own emotions and then, using my imagination, to transport these into the life situation and personality of the other person.

If we review the great tragedies of violence, racism, cruelty, discrimination, oppression and neglect that exist in our world today and throughout human history, we realize that these can exist only in the absence of empathy. The Golden Rule states "Do unto others as you would have done unto you." Clearly this is a statement of the need for empathy as a broad guide for our actions.

I want to grow in my ability to be a loving, empathetic person. However, I cannot empathize with other people's feelings if I'm not even aware of my own feelings. Lack of empathy leads to bluntness in communicating with others, a dehumanized, computerlike process I call fact-and-run communication, which pervades so many technical environments.

To develop our ability to be empathetic, we need to first become aware of our own emotions. Empathetic listening involves listening to the spoken words, the nonverbal expressions, the setting, and the silence (what is not said outright but implied, the emotional connotation of the words) of the person; and imagining that the same thing is happening to us under the same circumstances; and then realizing what emotions that event would elicit in us.

How Can Emotions Help Me or Hurt Me?

After reading about the emotions and knowing some of their properties, you may ask yourself the following question: How can emotions help me? What is their usefulness?

- They enhance our enjoyment, appreciation, and savoring of the good things of life: love, music, friendship, dance, nature, poetry, literature, painting, sculpture, cinema. They can make us more consciously aware of beauty and all its manifestations in nature and art, which can ultimately lead us to the source of all beauty, God.

- They tug on us, inviting us to respond to curiosity, awe, and wonder (Fuller 2006). They give us an awareness of the call of mystery, to enter into it and pursue it, as in human love, creativity, exploration, scientific research, and prayer.

- At the lowest level, emotions are essential for body survival and wellness. A quick knee-jerk response to physically threatening conditions. As our emotions teach us how to take care of our many needs, our growing empathy for others can also energize us to work for social justice.

- Emotions can act as an opposing balance to the use of pure reason, giving us a rounder, fuller, more balanced approach to reality.

- Emotions can warn us of danger or neglect. They establish priorities for action; they provide energy and direction for forward motion and for long-term perseverance in overcoming obstacles.

- Emotions are especially valuable guides for us in seeking, forming, and maintaining close relationships with others. They can give us an awareness of issues in our relating to other people: competition, jealousy, envy, prejudice, stereotyping, peer pressure, being excluded.

- Emotions help us organize our experiences by influencing what we attend to and helping us properly interpret events.

- Emotions are vitally needed as initiators of action, as life-givers, motivators, energizers. Emotions provide the basic fuel, the drive for human action. Scientific research itself requires a great amount of energizing emotions to initiate it, to overcome obstacles, and to stay with the research through difficulties and reversals.

  The depth, width, and richness with which you can participate in the many ways of experiencing and celebrating life—works of art, the beauty of nature, human friendships—depend strongly on your ability to be aware of your feelings.

- Emotions not recognized, accepted, or attended to can wreak havoc with your physical health, your relations, and your accurate perceptions of the events surrounding you.

On the negative side, emotions can become stuck in a long-term pattern, needing to be paid attention to and processed properly. We have to be aware of when an emotion has engulfed us and taken over control of our lives. Some danger signs of unhealthy emotions include compulsive eating, working, or shopping; dependence on alcohol or drugs; being stuck in a long-term emotion that saps our energy and does not go away; knee-jerk emotional outbursts.

> Self-knowledge decreases control from outside the person and increases control from within the person.
>
> —Abraham Maslow

Emotions for Self-Knowledge

As we go through our day, we need to keep developing our awareness of what emotions we're feeling at that time. We can say to ourselves "Right now, I feel afraid," or "As I talk to this person, I don't like her," or "I like my friend, but I also feel jealous of his success."

A strong emotional response, especially if it is unwarranted, usually can give us insight into our unconscious.

As we go through life, we need to get to know many people. Of all the people we need to know, the most important one is our very own self. We have a stranger living inside us! It takes a lifetime to get to know that stranger better, more intimately. To get to know that stranger within us, we need to be open to seeing our reflected image from other people and listening to what our emotions are telling us about ourselves. We need to develop a long-term habit of monitoring our emotions in order to increase our self-awareness, our self-knowledge.

The ancient Greek aphorism "Know thyself" is so true. We can unwittingly hurt others or ourselves because of our lack of self-awareness. With good self-awareness and self-knowledge, we can move forward in life and be much more effective in making sure that our intentions and our actions are in harmony with each other.

Human history is painfully full of people whose external actions and self-images were sadly out of sync with each other.

As we become aware of our fears, our prejudices, our anger, our mistrust, and our stereotyping of others, we can gain important insights into ourselves and also become more accepting of our own shortcomings and those of other people.

"It seems to me that clients who have moved significantly in therapy live more intimately with their feelings of pain, but also more vividly with their feelings of ecstasy; that anger is more clearly felt, but also is love; that fear is an experience they know more deeply, but so is courage. And the reason they can thus live fully in a wider range is that they have this underlying confidence in themselves as trustworthy instruments for encountering life" (Rogers 1961, 195).

Thematic Connection

Emotions are among the simplest, quickest, and most direct everyday ways to access our subconscious/unconscious (that part of our minds that we are not fully aware of yet have a great part in determining our beliefs and behavior).

If we are watching a movie or a program on TV and experience our stomach becoming tight, this is a good time to stop and reflect: What theme is going on in that story we are watching that is common to a theme from our past that we have a strong emotional reaction to? We will learn to communicate with ourselves while gaining valuable self-knowledge if we take the time to do this exercise.

A trigger event is anything in the present that reminds us of a special event in our past. It can be a sight, a smell, a taste, a place or setting, a person, a situation. For someone who has PTSD, a trigger event can bring strong flashbacks and a reexperiencing of some aspects of the original trauma. PTSD is not limited to war veterans, but includes anyone who had an unusually painful experience in the past (Matsakis 1992).

- Personal association or thematic connection: two events or settings are related when they have a common or similar theme.

(Theme of present event) = (Theme of trigger event in my past)

If we wish to live healthy emotional lives, it is really important that we take in the concept of a theme and learn how to apply it to life situations. Theme is the central and unifying concept of a story.

Let's work with an analogy in order to better understand the mechanism of a trigger event. Let's say we are faced with a chemical sample whose chemical composition we want to know. One way to find out the chemical composition of the sample is to radiate it with different wavelengths, while observing which particular wavelengths are absorbed by the sample. Absorption indicates the presence of a particular chemical element or compound in the sample. By looking at the wavelength absorption peaks of the sample, we can identify its chemical composition. An analogy to this occurs in the human mind: when something happens in our present lives (a trigger event) that resonates with an important content in our unconscious, we will react by experiencing a strong emotion.

When we experience a strong emotional response to an event in our present lives, if we can identify its theme, this will put us in touch with an important theme in our unconscious minds. Being aware of our emotions helps us look for these "absorption resonant peaks" and gives us insight into the contents of our unconscious minds.

Emotional Intelligence

Given that we have all these emotions inside us strongly influencing our behavior, what do we need to work toward in self-knowledge? How do we know what is necessary? There are five characteristics of emotional intelligence (Goleman 1995, 315; Bradberry and Greaves 2003, 23 and 28–32):

1. Knowledge of one's emotions: having self-awareness, recognizing a feeling as it happens. There is a mystery person living inside of you. This is a part of the real you, the you behind all your external masks and the roles you play. Paying continuing long-term attention to your emotions as they arise will enable you to be more truly you as you grow spiritually, leading to self-knowledge, which can lead to self-acceptance. Being aware of your emotions does not imply that you then dump them on the person you are talking to!

This above all: to thine own self be true, and
it must follow, as the night the day, thou canst
not then be false to any man.
—Hamlet

2. Managing emotions: handling feelings so they are appropriate. We have knee-jerk emotional responses that can short-circuit our personal growth. Managing these requires that we stay focused while keeping in check inappropriately strong or deficient emotional responses. We seek to feel the emotion while not letting it overpower us so as to become more steadily balanced in all our undertakings.

3. Motivating oneself: marshaling emotions in the service of a goal. Emotional self-control, delaying gratification, being persistent, stifling impulsiveness. To carry out any project requires start-up energy, steady follow-through, and an active response to overcoming barriers in our way.

4. Recognizing emotions in others: being attuned to the subtle social signals that indicate what the other person needs or wants. To be able to love others, we need to be sensitive to their individual needs, paying careful attention to their nonverbal language. We have already seen what happened in history when Galileo did not take into account the emotions of Pope Urban VIII!

> Unless you can listen to my silence, you will never understand my words.
> —Anonymous

5. Handling relationships: interacting smoothly with others. Staying sensitive, alert, and observant as we interact with others. Being on the lookout to avoid trip wires, knee-jerk turnoffs to the way we interact with others.

Therapist Carl Rogers discusses the challenge of acknowledging and properly identifying our emotions:

In the realm of feelings, we have never learned to attach symbols [identify and give names] to experience with any accuracy of meaning. This something which I feel welling up in myself, in the safety of an acceptant relationship—what is it? Is it sadness, is it anger, is it regret, is it sorry for myself, is it anger at lost opportunities—I stumble around trying out a wide range of symbols, until one fits, feels right, seems really to fit my actual experience. In doing this type of thing the client discovers that he has to learn the language of feeling and emotion as if you were an infant learning to speak; often even worse, he finds he must unlearn a false language before learning the true one (Rogers 1961, 204).

Accessing Your Emotions

One of two ways to be aware of your emotions is to stay tuned in to your body all throughout the day. You will discover that your body has a characteristic way of responding to emotions: muscle tension, upset stomach, headache, grinding teeth, forming fists, blurred vision, and so on. Learn to listen to your body when it signals you that an emotion is present, then reflect on what happened just previously and work on it until you realize what that emotion was and what triggered it.

> Man is affected not by events but by the view
> he takes of them.
> —Epictetus (AD 55–135)

Joke: A man is staying at an exclusive metropolitan hotel. Very loud piano music keeps coming through the wall from next door. The man calls the main desk and complains angrily. The hotel manager responds, "Oh, that's a famous visiting piano performer. He is practicing for tonight's concert at the Opera House." The man says politely "Oh, never mind!" and he sits down to enjoy the music. This incident illustrates how our emotional responses can be affected by our belief system. Some people call this *ABC* (Ellis 2004).

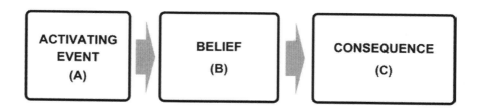

Figure 16 ABC theory of emotions

A is the activating event, *B* is the belief, and *C* is the consequence. *B*, my belief system, is somewhat under my control. If I believe that everybody should be nice to me, I'm going to experience many unnecessary upsets throughout my day.

Using the *ABC* model, you will find that useful insights will follow when you reflect on the activating event *A*, the belief *B*, and the consequent emotion evoked *C*. It is important to realize that you have control over *B*, your belief system. For example, "People should always take my feelings into account" is a belief system that can bring on much unnecessary suffering.

A second way of growing in awareness of your emotions is to keep an emotions diary. As you go through your normal day, notice which emotions you are feeling at that moment and write them down quickly. At a later time, reflect on your notes in order to see what they tell you about yourself, especially if you can observe recurring patterns of the same emotional response. Pay special attention to severe responses that can indicate that PTSD has been activated by a trigger event (Matsakis 1992).

After you spend some time noticing your emotions and responding to them, you may find it helpful as a tool to personify these emotions as they act in you.

For example, choose a character from a story or movie who personifies anger for you, and use that character whenever you talk about your anger. Likewise, choose a character from a story or movie for every one of the other emotions you have been able to identify in yourself.

After doing some reflecting on your emotions, you may find you can only go so far. In working with emotions, it helps to talk them over with another person. The act of describing your emotions and responding to questions from your friend will help you verbalize a more accurate image of what emotion(s) are at hand.

Personal Reflections

I'm glad that I have invested the time and effort to become aware of and at home with my emotions. Time well spent. I am more accepting of myself and of others. Less hitting my head on brick walls.

Exercises

- Keep a feelings diary. Carry a notebook with you all throughout the day, and note in it the emotional reactions you are aware of as the day progresses. As you continue doing this, you will notice that the number of emotions and the subtle differences among them can become clearer to you. You will also note if you have an emotion or emotions that constantly recur and need paying attention to.

- While watching a movie or video, choose an actor and write down the feelings that actor might be experiencing as the action progresses in the story.

- Review key events in your life (both good and bad). What emotions did you experience at those times?

- How do you respond to your emotions in a positive, constructive way?

- How do you respond to your emotions in a negative, destructive way? Does an emotion ever engulf you, taking away your self-control?

- What emotions are hard for you to acknowledge in yourself?

- Take the list of emotions shown and for each category, find an instance in your life when you experienced that emotion.

- Is any single emotion habitual to you?

- Choose a person who is close to you and observe the emotions expressed or not expressed by him or her.

- What are some of your trigger events?

In keeping your emotions log throughout the day, note not only the emotions you feel, but also what body sensations have made you aware of that particular emotion. Here is a suggested table in which you can record for each emotion how it manifests itself in your body.

By carrying out these exercises, you are actually building up your unique emotions dictionary to allow you to transform your body sensations into an awareness of which emotion is acting within you at that time. I find it helpful to be on the lookout for my habitual knee-jerk compulsive responses. When I experience a compulsion coming out (eating, working, reading, etc.), I reflect on what has just happened to me, and many times, I can pinpoint the emotions that are acting within me at that point and what triggered them.

Emotions Checklist

When you become aware of experiencing an emotion during your everyday life, write down reflections on each event.

1. What event triggered me?
2. Did I experience any sensations in my body?
3. Any recurrent compulsive response?

Emotion Experienced

Anger:

Fear:

Jealousy:

Envy:

Joy:

Anxiety:

Sadness:

Shame:

Wonder:

Love:

Chapter 7
Achieving Deep, Quality Relations with Others

It is impossible to define human beings without showing them in relationships with others. It is no accident that the second-worst punishment for a crime short of execution is to place a person in solitary confinement. We desperately need others in order to grow.

Machine Communication

People trained in science can have a clearly predefined image of what technical communication entails: we have a transmitter, we have a transmission medium, and we have a receiver. The transmitter and the receiver have a formal set of rules accepted ahead of time regarding transmission format and also the unique meaning assigned to the codes being transmitted. For digital communication, ones and zeros combine to form patterns that can be found in a table that tells us precisely what the meaning of the transmitted message is at that moment.

Code	Meaning
00	0
01	1
10	2
11	3

Interpersonal communication is a lot broader, richer, and more complex than communication between two machines. Since our spirituality is deeply affected by our relatedness to other people, our fluency and sensitivity in interpersonal communication is vital to us. It is important that we understand the many nuances involved in human communication.

Interactive Dialogue

In the machine communication example above, the information flows in one predetermined direction. I visualize machine communication as a one-way arrow. Human communication, on the other hand, is more of a constantly evolving interactive dialogue. I find it helpful to visualize interpersonal communication as being like going to a dance and, for some reason, all of a sudden being paired up to dance with a total stranger. Total control is impossible. You have to pay attention to the other; a constant adaptive give-and-take interaction goes through the whole process. Constant learning and accommodation need to take place for both people involved in the dance.

When two people converse, the message at hand cannot be determined totally by any one sender only. Such is human communication.

Contrasting Machine Versus Human Communication

Machine: modular connections with interchangeable components.
Interpersonal: no two persons the same. People have different backgrounds, attitudes, expectations, values.

Machine: predictable, controlled behavior.
Interpersonal: take tentative steps, one at a time, staying open to the response received.

Machine: finite list of code entries is allowed.

Interpersonal: open-ended exchange possible, no limits. Nonverbal communication is an essential part of the interaction.

Machine: previously agreed-upon meaning of code is used exclusively.

Interpersonal: personal associations can overpower the intended messages at any time.

Machine: transmitter sends one-way message to receiver.

Interpersonal: simultaneous, interactive, time-varying, two-way dialogue is taking place, whether intended or not.

Nonverbal Communication

Interpersonal communication has been studied for decades, and researchers have found that the communication process between two people contains a large percentage of nonverbal information. The results of years of research show that two-thirds of all communication taking place between two people is nonverbal.

Nonverbal communication between humans has no equivalent in the world of machine-to-machine communication. This presents a challenge to those of us who have technical training because we're used to identifying the content of a communication totally, exclusively with the signs that were transmitted. So, what is nonverbal communication?

Nonverbal communication is made up of all the factors that convey information yet are not part of the spoken speech. This includes, but is not limited to, the following:

- Tone of voice, volume, pitch.
- Presence or absence of eye contact.
- Facial expressions: anger, guilt, fear, grimacing, threatening look, avoidance actions.
- Physical setting: the actual place where two people are communicating affects the content and tone of the communication. Talking to somebody in your living room is different than carrying on the same conversation inside a courtroom or a hospital corridor. A conversation taking place in your cubicle will have a different bias than if it took place in your boss's office.
- Position: sitting, standing, looking down from above, looking up from below, turning away.
- Body posture.
- As a person, what I say can be just as important as what I don't say. Absence of speech also communicates. Physical absence communicates.
- When the verbal and the nonverbal messages disagree, the receiver will then tend to believe the nonverbal message first. Children will also "hear" our nonverbal messages even when these contradict our well-intended verbal preaching.
- Individuals are aware of little of their own nonverbal behavior, which is enacted mindlessly, spontaneously, and unconsciously...We respond to gestures with an extreme alertness and, one might almost say, in accordance with an elaborate and secret code that is written nowhere, known to none and understood by all (Samovar and Porter 2000).

Everyday Interactions

Have you ever had the unpleasant experience of totally miscommunicating with another person, with many hurts resulting? Let's remember that words have emotional connotations, some of them possessing very strong or even overwhelming energy. Thus, a message sent can elicit different (subjective) responses from different people. The speaker can generate a message without really having full awareness of all the nuances of meaning (denotations and connotations) of that message. The listener will interpret the message according to his or her own subjective life experience and actually perceive receiving a message that may be completely different from what was intended by the transmitter.

We now have an unusual situation with the transmitter sending a message that he or she doesn't have full awareness of, and the receiver is getting a message that could be completely different from what the transmitter intended.

Connotations/Personal Associations

It's important to remember that the words used in human language contain several dictionary meanings, or denotations, and can also trigger personal, highly emotional connotations in the receiver. Besides the public dictionary we can all refer to, we all carry personal dictionaries within us that reflect our painful or sensitive experiences from the past. Our nonverbal message can act as a trigger capable of energizing a PTSD response in the listener.

> If you don't understand my silence, you will
> never understand my words.
> —Anonymous

Love is the only way to grasp another human being in the innermost core of his personality. No one can become fully aware of the very essence of another human being unless he loves him. By his love he is enabled to see the essential traits and features in the beloved person; and even more, he sees that which is potential in him, which is not yet actualized but yet ought to be actualized. Furthermore, by his love, the loving person enables the beloved person to actualize these potentialities. By making him aware of what he can be and of what he should become, he makes these potentialities come true (Frankel 1959, 134).

Masculine and Feminine

A considerable amount of research has been carried out comparing communication styles among different groups. Work done since the 1980s found that there are important differences between the way women and men communicate. I find the following table extremely helpful; I find I need to refer back to it over and over again to check my communication style. The physical sciences, the technical schools, and high-tech industry tend to be strongly masculine in orientation. For those of us immersed in a very masculine work environment all day long, it is a challenge to leave work and then change our communication styles.

A work environment that values highly focused goals, schedules, and productivity leads to what I like to call fact-and-run communication. The nurturing of human relationships at home and with our friends requires attentive listening, time, effort, dialogue, and empathy instead. Masculine and feminine, we need both!

> Women's liberation is the liberation of the
> feminine in the man and the masculine in the
> woman.
>
> —Corita Kent

"Civilization is almost exclusively masculine, a civilization of power in which woman has been thrust aside in the shade. Therefore, it has lost its balance and is moving by hopping from war to war...This one-sided civilization is crashing along a series of catastrophes at a tremendous speed because of its one-sidedness" (Tagore 2007, 431).

"Many generalizations could be made about the history of the Western mind, but today perhaps the most immediately obvious is that it has been from start to finish an overwhelmingly masculine phenomenon...The crisis of modern man is an essentially masculine crisis, and I believe that his resolution is already now occurring in the tremendous emergence of the feminine in our culture" (Tarnas 1991, 441).

The psychologist Carl Jung spent decades giving therapy to a large number of people from many different backgrounds. In reflecting on his observations of his patients, he came up with some very pertinent concepts. He noted that there were two different forms of human consciousness: feminine (anima) and masculine (animus). A woman will tend to have a consciousness that is predominantly feminine, with a less developed masculine side. A man will tend to have a consciousness that is predominantly masculine, with a less developed feminine side. Jung concluded that in the first half of life, we develop one mode predominantly, while the other one will be less developed. The task of the second half of life is the integration of both modes of consciousness in ourselves.

- Masculine consciousness: logical, argumentative, rational, analytic, thinking, abstract, categorizing, judgmental, aggressive, out of touch with the unconscious.

- Feminine consciousness: poetic, intuitive, feeling, imagistic, imaginative, relational, nonclassifying, affirming, receptive, close to the unconscious.

Those of us working in a high-tech environment need to carefully select which of these two modes of relating we choose at any time: masculine for projects requiring a high level of discipline, feminine when in a caring relationship.

Here is a table (Samovar and Porter 2000, 174) that can be used to sensitize us as to what mode of relational communication we are using at any time. I find I have to return to this table time after time. This table was originally used to describe differences between feminine and masculine communication styles, but it can also be used to contrast impersonal, results-oriented workplace communication with that needed for close relationships.

The overriding theme of feminine talk is seeking relationship. The overriding themes of masculine talk are power and results orientation.

1. **Feminine talk:** Use talk to build and sustain rapport with others.

Masculine talk: Use talk to assert yourself and your ideas.

2. **Feminine talk:** Share yourself and learn about others through disclosing.

Masculine talk: Personal disclosure can make you vulnerable.

3. **Feminine talk:** Use talk to create symmetry or equality between people.

Masculine talk: Use talk to establish your status and power.

4. **Feminine talk:** Matching experience with others shows understanding and empathy. ("I know how you feel.")

Masculine talk: Matching experiences is a competitive strategy to command attention. ("I can top that.")

5. **Feminine talk:** To support others, express understanding of their feelings.

Masculine talk: To support others, do something helpful—give advice or solve a problem for them.

6. **Feminine talk:** Include others in conversation by asking their opinions and encouraging them to elaborate. Wait your turn to speak so others can participate.

Masculine talk: Don't share the talk stage with others; wrest it from them with communication. Interrupt others to make your own points.

7. **Feminine talk:** Keep the conversation going by asking questions and showing interest in others' ideas.

Masculine talk: Each person is on his or her own; it's not your job to help others join in.

8. **Feminine talk:** Be responsive. Let others know you hear and care about what they say.

Masculine talk: Use responses to make your own points and to outshine others.

9. **Feminine talk:** Be tentative, so that others feel free to add their ideas.

Masculine talk: Be assertive, so others perceive you as confident and in command.

10. **Feminine talk:** Talking is a human relationship in which details and interesting side comments enhance depth of connection.

Masculine talk: Talking is a linear sequence that should convey information and accomplish goals. Extraneous details get in the way and achieve nothing.

The Languages of Spirituality

At this point you may ask yourself, "What is included in language?" I find it helpful to define language as anything that can cause a change to take place in me.

Music has a capacity to move us very deeply, so it is very definitely a part of language. Whenever I try to express my personal experience of falling in love, I can't help but be drawn back to the opera *La Boheme* when Rodolfo meets Mimi for the first time, and as they start to fall in love, they sing the duet *"Che Gelida Manina"* (What a cold little hand). Rodolfo and Mimi are not individual people; they are acting as carriers of the universal experience of the first encounter between two lovers! I thank God for people like Giacomo Puccini who had the insight, sensitivity, talent, and determination to help express for us the inexpressible.

> Music expresses that which cannot be said
> and on which it is impossible to be silent.
> —Victor Hugo

Quality literature and poetry can reveal some of the depths of human experience and express it in terms that we need to borrow from the great artists. Sculptures and paintings have the capacity to move us, so they are also language. The way a person treats me by being present to me or by ignoring me affects me at great depths; this also constitutes language.

I need to open up, to amplify my conception of language. I need to move beyond the strict, sharp, literal definitions of mathematics and move on into a new field that is boundless, that includes all human facial expressions, architecture, cinema, music, sculpture, painting, music, literature, poetry, touch, dance, proximity, and presence.

We need to cultivate art and all its forms in order to extend our ability to express ourselves, to explore the world of spirituality.

The vast range of human experiences far outstrips our written or spoken vocabularies.

Johari Window

Have you ever had the experience of observing a friend act in a way that was totally surprising to you? Have you ever done something that was out of character as seen by you and others? We all have both public and private parts to us. The Johari Window (Luft and Ingham 1955) is a tool that helps us visualize the four possible ways of having knowledge about ourselves. Picture a window made up of four windowpanes. The total window represents all that there is to ever know or not know about you: your likes and dislikes, your goals, your life history, your secrets, your needs, your fantasies, everything.

There are things you know about yourself and things you do not know about yourself. Likewise, there are things others know about you and things others do not know about you. All in all, there are four possible combinations which we can visualize as being four panes in a window:

    1. Known to others and also to myself (open)

    2. Known to others but not to myself (my blind spots)

3. I know but others do not know (private)

4. Unknown to everyone (mystery)

As we grow, we can have *Aha!* moments when we discover new insights about ourselves that we had no awareness of before. This process of self-discovery never ends! The boundary between these two regions, my self-knowledge and my lack of self-knowledge, should keep on changing if I am open to growth.

Part 1—Known to others and to myself (open)

This includes the information about you that both you and the other person are aware of, your public face.

This area will tend to contain the shallowest, most obvious information about you: your name, age, gender, ethnicity, appearance, place of work, address, characteristic outward behavior, and so on. Also included are your conscious actions and statements. You are in partial control of what is in this space, since you can choose what you will disclose to others here. Most everyday transactions between people fall into this region.

Part 2—Known to others, but not to myself (my blind spots)

This section represents the information about you that the other person knows, but you are unaware of. These are your personal blind spots, which can be obvious to others but not to yourself.

Reading about major human events throughout history and the leaders who made it happen, it becomes obvious that many of these leaders, in spite of their intelligence, strength, resolve, power, and abilities, had some serious blind spots that ultimately proved to be their undoing.

Our conscious actions, decisions, and energies can make great things happen in life. Simultaneously, our blind spots have just as much strength, tenacity, and capacity to limit us and to hurt us and those around us. We can hurt or limit the lives of our loved ones without being aware of what we are doing at all.

Let's make an analogy. How do I know what my face looks like? It's impossible for me to see my own face unless I have a reflecting surface: a mirror or a pond. Likewise, it is very difficult to gain self-knowledge without another human being reflecting back to me what's in my blind area. For me to see my blind area, I need to take in feedback and insights from another person. This illustrates how much I need to be in a close, trusting relationship with someone else in order to be able to grow as a human being. All our schooling and all our efforts to know ourselves will always fall short without help from trusted friends.

We need to cultivate quality friendships, friendships that go beyond polite niceties and superficialities. We desperately need to create a safe space, then share intimacies with one another within that space. Always be selective as to who you share personal information with. Sharing personal information with a colleague at work has some hazards to it, since it can make you vulnerable to being hurt at a later time.

A second source of self-knowledge involves journaling. We need to take time out and write down our day-to-day experiences, reflecting on them and what they say about us. Journaling is a compassionate, soul-searching look at what our behavior and our feelings reveal about our true selves, the strangers within. (See chapter 9).

Journaling should never be harsh or critical. We need to develop self-love, accepting ourselves as we are, not as some perfect model would demand of us. Your journal should always be totally private. Never let anyone read it, not even someone close to you. Once you have an awareness that your writing will be read by someone else, your inner critic will immediately cramp your style as you begin worrying about your public image, not hurting others' feelings, the correct spelling of words, and sentence structure. A journal has to be totally spontaneous, without censorship! Allow yourself to misspell words, neglect to cross the *t*'s or dot the *i*'s. Allow yourself to swear or exaggerate. Keep your journal well secured. You have the option to shred pages of your journal on an ongoing basis as needed.

Part 3—Known to me only (private)

This represents the part of yourself that you are unwilling to share with anyone at all. Self-protection, fear of being hurt, and shame keep us from sharing this information. A setting of trust is needed before we can share this part of ourselves with others. It is a sign of the depth and quality of a relationship when we can share this material. "Why am I afraid to tell you who I am? Because if you knew me, you would not like me" (Powell 1969).

It is paradoxical but true that you know yourself to the extent that you are known. Your thoughts, feelings, and needs often remain vague and clouded until you put them into words. Expressing your needs, for example, gives them shape and color, adds details, and points out inconsistencies and possible areas of conflict that you need to resolve (McKay, Davis, and Fanning 1995).

Part 4—Unknown to everyone (mystery)

This region represents information that is unknown to you and to all others. We are mysteries to others as well as to ourselves! We discover some of our hidden talents, dark sides, and depths only gradually as we grow in life while being open to acquiring self-knowledge.

In order to get to know ourselves, we need to put time aside to reflect on our life experiences and to expose ourselves to good stories and art. For access to narratives, scriptures are preferred because they were written at a time when story was used as a means of teaching, not entertaining. In the case of art, don't be intimidated by art critics or by galleries to value a particular *ism* school of art. You choose the art that touches you. Avoid constant-stimulation entertainment and sensationalism or short-attention-span fads; you will recognize good art as you feel it touching you with the ring of truth, opening you, healing you, giving a voice to your inner being. Set time aside to meditate on this worthwhile art.

Keeping a depth journal helps us to reflect on our daily experiences and to grow in self-knowledge. When we don't reflect, we can wind up running through life blaming others for all our misfortunes.

The four panes of the Johari window are not meant to be rigid. To the extent that we are open to life, growth, and self-examination, we can make those boundaries move. A good part of spiritual growth consists of being aware of those boundaries and then working to move them in the right direction, toward greater openness, self-knowledge, acceptance, and self-love. As we grow in self-knowledge, we should naturally grow in acceptance and compassion toward others.

Martin Buber

Martin Buber was a Jewish philosopher who lived in the twentieth century. He generated some ideas about human relatedness and communication that are very broad, simple, and incisive. He wrote a classic book called *I and Thou* (Buber 1937). I like the insights that Buber's thoughts give me. They make me stop to think about how I am relating to other people. Here they are. See what you think.

Buber said that, broadly speaking, we can relate to another person in one of three ways: I-it, I-you, and I-thou.

I-It

In an I-it relationship, I relate to the other person by treating him or her in a broad, impersonal way, only concerned with his or her generic function in my life. The other person is just an object to me. This attitude is a natural outcome of living in a depersonalized high-density area, of worker mobility, of specialization. All these factors tend to force human relations to become practical, results oriented, modular, and dehumanized. Whenever I use an ATM, I am tangibly reminded of an I-it relationship.

Figure 17 Martin Buber

Examples of people who might fit into an I-it relationship: the cashier, the fetus, the secretary, the homeless person, the purchasing agent, the terrorist, the foreigner, the illegal immigrant.

This I-it mode is intentionally emphasized in military training in order to enable soldiers to shoot to kill an anonymous enemy instead of dealing with a unique human being who has a life history, feelings, and a real-life family waiting for him back home.

When we treat a person as an *it*, the process tends to self-reinforce: "Insofar as I see him [the patient in therapy] only as an

176

object, the client will tend to become only an object" (Rogers 1961, 201).

I-You

In an I-you relationship, I recognize the unique identity of the other person. This particular person has a recognizable personality and a unique life history, likes and dislikes.

Examples of I-you:

- Grocery store cashier Janice in checkout lane three who had a bad back last week and carries pictures of her grandchildren with her. She smiles and remembers us by name every time we go through her checkout lane.
- Hairstylist June who is a refugee from Vietnam and collects food once a month to give to the poor.
- Secretary Elizabeth who is a very special compassionate listener at work. She used to play the organ in her church. Her taste in music runs to Elvis and old-time Spirituals.

I-Thou

In an I-thou relationship, I am aware of the person carrying the image of God (thou) in his or her unique, God-given personhood. This is based on a Judeo-Christian belief that is called *imago Dei* (Latin expression for *image of God*).

The Hebrew Bible describes the creation of the first human beings using symbolic language. This symbolic language alludes to all humans having great dignity while carrying Godlike qualities like rationality, creativity, love, and relatedness.

Please note that *image of God* includes all human beings, not just people of our race or background or same beliefs or people we feel comfortable with!

177

Then God said, "Let us make humankind in our image, according to our likeness; and let them have dominion over the fish of the sea, and over the birds of the air, and over the cattle, and over all the wild animals of the earth, and over every creeping thing that creeps upon the earth. So, God created humankind in his image, in the image of God he created them; male and female he created them.

—Genesis 1:26–27

Any man's death diminishes me, because I am involved in mankind; and therefore, never send to know for whom the bell tolls; it tolls for thee.　　　　—John Dunne

When I recognize that the person in front of me has been created purposefully by a loving God, carrying in him- or herself some of God's attributes of creativity, relationship, rationality, and ability to love, then I am called to cherish the special value of this person.

I am having a hard time coming up with examples for this one! Somehow platitudes just don't cut it. I think of the famous American psychologist William James who did an experimental study of people who claimed to have had mystical experiences of God (James 1902). One common characteristic of all their experiences was that the experience was ineffable (i.e., it could not be verbalized, in spite of being very real and very powerful to them and having a great impact on their lives). Maybe this is why I'm having a hard time verbalizing this.

This I-thou relatedness can be clearly seen in the works of Mother Theresa, Martin Luther King, Mahatma Gandhi, Cesar Chavez, Desmond Tutu and many, many others.

- The experience of a tiny newborn baby when he or she first can focus his or her eyes, and he or she experiences the warm, loving gaze of an adult welcoming him or her.
- Anne Frank in her famous quote that "In spite of everything, I still believe that people are really good at heart."
- Mother Theresa, who spent her adult life taking care of the outcasts, the "untouchables" of India.

Any person, group, movement, or country who oppresses, enslaves, discriminates against, exploits, or does violence to others is violating the *imago Dei* quality belonging to all human beings. (*All* includes people different from me—people I may not like!)

Reflections

- Who do you routinely relate to as an *it*?
- Who do you routinely relate to as a *you*?
- Who do you routinely relate to as a *thou*?
- Describe some contents in each of your four personal Johari window panes.
- Describe personal incidents of miscommunicating with another person.
- Describe some of your communicating styles, one for your work environment and one for close relations.
- Describe the nonverbal language of close friends.
- Describe some aspects of your own nonverbal language.
- What nonverbal behavior in others can push your buttons?
- Do you remember a loved one entering into loving dialogue with you? Feeling special and cared for? Having your special needs acknowledged and valued?
- Make a list of your perception of the greatest needs of your close loved ones and resolve to act upon this.
- How did it feel when someone ignored you totally as if you weren't there?
- How did it feel when someone talked at you without including you or being aware of your feelings?
- What do you do to increase your self-knowledge?
- What types of people do you have the most difficult time with?
- Make a mental list of people whom you trust enough to share your true inner self with.
- What parts of yourself do you withhold in prayer?

For Further Reading

Adler, Ronald, and George Rodman. 1991. *Understanding Human Communication*. Austin, TX: Holt, Rinehart and Winston.

Chapter 8
Moving Forward: Obstacles to Overcome

Concept of the Self

We have seen how a metaphor can be used to describe the unknown in terms of the known, the familiar. Metaphors, especially ones that are used extensively or have been around for a long time, can take on a life of their own, leading us to unconsciously take them to be literally and universally true. We can experience some difficulty distancing ourselves from these well-established metaphors when it becomes necessary to do so. Here is a list of some currently popular metaphors that can drastically affect our self-image, setting a glass ceiling on our aspirations, as was so aptly described in the story of the ugly duckling who thought he would never rise above his environment.

- "Humans are animals." Even though we do share many features in common with animals, a small amount of introspection on our human culture and its many achievements will show you we possess superior qualities that are completely out of the reach of other animals.

- "The universe is nothing but a machine made up exclusively of matter, which behaves in a mechanical, predetermined way." Humans have qualities that are not machinelike: seeking purpose, some freedom of choice, loving relatedness, creativity.

- "The human mind is a computer." Our minds are much richer than any computer. We possess some free will, a moral sense, an appreciation of beauty, creativity, and the capacity to love. Computers, on the other hand, no matter how impressive their capabilities may be, can only slavishly follow directions given to them by their human programmers.

- "The human body is a biochemical machine." Our bodies respond to chemical intervention via medicines, yet the placebo effect is well known: sometimes patients who are given an inert tablet for treatment will have a perceived or actual improvement in a medical condition. This effect shows we are more than just chemicals, since our minds can influence our bodies' response to drugs. When new drugs are undergoing clinical testing, great efforts are spent in avoiding the placebo effect (the patient's mind affecting his or her body's response), which could result in false research outcomes. Chemicals do not experience the placebo effect!

- I find it helpful to limit my expectations about science. Science is a useful, limited tool only. Science becomes a false god when we expect too much from it.

Reject pessimistic, machinelike pictures of humanity and all their context of depersonalization and being less than, with its associated gloom. Move forward with a positive spirit, proud to be human, in awe at the wonder of being human.

Let go of hopes of unifying all human knowledge under the umbrella of science; live in a diversity of many voices comfortably. To quote Robert Bellah, "We will recognize the multiplicity of the human spirit, and the necessity to translate constantly between different scientific and imaginative vocabularies." (Tarnas 1991, 416).

Acknowledge the limitations of science; stop waiting for it to have all the answers. Life is not a problem to be solved, but a mystery to be lived.

Our Subjective Selves

Over the years I have enjoyed the company of many friends who are active in the arts and humanities. Over and over again, I have been surprised to notice how comfortable they seemed to be with their subjective appraisal of things. I, on the other hand, have had trouble trusting my subjective feelings. I noticed that I had a common response when I was faced with interpretations of history, works of art, and world events. I felt guilty, feeling the need to find an equation or some universal principle to provide me with *the* answer: the unique, solid, inescapable answer.

- My engineering schooling trained me to distrust and turn off my subjective self, to ignore my emotions. (I didn't even know they were there in the first place or that they had anything to contribute to the process.)

- The answer to any problem needed to come inexorably from some principle, some equation that was bigger than me. All I had to do was to find that principle and to then apply it.

Regardless of my unique life history and storehouse of experience, I expected that I should get the same results to a given problem as anyone else. If we both didn't get the same answer, one of us was in error and had to change. The idea that reality might be multidimensional and could be approached using many distinct voices was difficult for me to accept. When I looked at a work of art, I became suspicious of its value since I noticed that other people walked away from it with different interpretations of it than I did.

My love for art kept me moving forward. I took several studio art classes. I did drawing and painting. As I "thawed out" a bit, I realized that art can evoke a response, instead of forcing a unique literal message on the viewer. The same work of art will evoke different responses even in me at different times as my life experience grows.

Our response to a work of art describes us as much as it does the work. Art touches our unconscious. We project (Mattoon 1981, 126) parts of our unconscious onto the work. Art helps us get in closer contact with our unconscious that way.

- Statements in science seek to converge sharply to a unique interpretation.

- Artistic statements can evoke multiple, dynamic, evolving, personal responses from us.

I have spent many years working in industrial research departments in different companies. As the years went by and as I gained more and more experience in my own technical field, I observed and I concluded that the phrase "experts agree that..." is overstated. If we were to convene a group of experts in a closed meeting room to resolve a problem in their field of expertise, chances are that they would argue interminably, maybe the most vocal one eventually winning out.

I realized that the veneer of science being the only way to answer questions had become a security blanket for me, some release from personal responsibility and from experiencing uncertainty.

Over and over again, life thrust personal and family problems at me, which negated my objectivity and my status as a separate detached observer.

- I became intricately enmeshed in living, loving, and struggling with relational problems that drew me into themselves; required an impassioned involvement; and in many cases, required that I change, that I grow to meet the new challenges facing me.

We only grow when we are open to life and we respond to its challenges with openness. When we disclaim responsibility; act as detached, objective observers; or refuse to accept our part in the problem, people we love can experience abandonment, get hurt, or be held back in their personal growth.

Our subjective selves are influenced by our life histories, our temperaments, the cultures and lived experiences of our ancestors.

- Our subjective selves contain a good amount of "Why? Just because! That's why!"

It's important to acknowledge, value, cherish, and embrace our subjective, unique selves instead of always waiting for an answer from outside ourselves. When we embrace our uniqueness, this does not mean we should allow ourselves to become self-willed or rigid; on the contrary, staying fluid and open is still important. As we struggle finding our own way, it's helpful to stay open to reason and experience plus advice from others we value. The object is to become more truly ourselves.

Of all the seven billion people living on Earth, you have a unique life history. Your family of origin was a unique blend of two family lines. Your mother and father themselves had unique life environments and experiences. Wars, economic hardships, relocations, separations, deaths, national upheavals, culture shock, disorientation, loss of status. All these events leave a lasting impact on our personalities. It is of paramount importance that we learn to accept our subjective selves!

- There is no book or expert who has a narrow, detailed answer to your unique life situation. The buck stops here!

The founder of humanistic psychology, Abraham Maslow, was quoted as saying "I have learned more about human nature by being married and raising a family than I had learned from all my studies in Psychology" (Hoffman 1992).

To be human means to:
- Possess a unique life history
- Be many- faceted
- Experience constant, dynamic inner changes
- Be self-contradictory at times
- Not be totally self-aware
- Seek loving relatedness
- Be unable to fully express our deeper parts

Scientific and technical work always seeks to be objective. The result of a research project should always be independent of the person achieving that result. Spirituality, on the other hand, strongly includes the subjective part of the person. Throughout my spiritual life, my unique background will always remain present and active. Your spirituality will always carry your unique "fingerprint," never totally the same as anyone else's. There is a spiritual entitled "Just as I Am." I love that title; it reminds me of the fact that I am not a generic abstraction. I have a unique life history and personality. I desperately need to be loved just the way I am. Without self-acceptance, it is hard to move forward in life.

We have to constantly acknowledge, accept, and work with our uniqueness! Awareness of both our talents and our limitations is important. Being aware of our talents allows us to choose activities in which we can help others. Evaluating our interactions with others, our relationship or lack of relationship with God, our fears, our prejudices, our irrational beliefs, our "brick walls," and our knee-jerk reactions requires spending time reviewing our lives. This is the stuff of which our unique spiritual lives are made. God accepts me just as I am; it takes concerted effort to get to know that unique person I am.

Suggestions

- Make a list of people who have hurt you. Keep this list and make a resolve to move to a point of compassion where you can forgive these people one by one. It takes a lot of energy and concentration to stay angry at those who have hurt us; forgiveness heals us and liberates us to use the same energies to move forward. It also releases these people from the prison of our hatred, opening us to love them the way they are and the way they need to be loved.

- Make a list of people you have hurt, either actively or indirectly by withholding your love. Resolve to make reparations as best as you can. Learn to forgive yourself!

- Make a list of the people who acknowledged you, loved you, were role models for you. Keep these people present in your mind as resources to imitate. I find it helpful to keep photos posted near my workspace of both public heroes and the people who have really touched my life at close range. I can look at a photograph I've had for decades and see new depths in it as I have more life experience and hopefully, have matured some more.

- Identify gaps in your early life, in your studies, and in your professional life that are holding you back from full spiritual growth. Work on filling those gaps as best you can.

- Reflect: Do you have elements in your worldview that set a glass ceiling on your aspirations?

Standardization Versus Individual Needs

One of the principles that gives technology its great power is the ability to standardize products so they will all behave in the same way. Standards are defined for system performance and for modular interconnection. Both hardware and software require totally predictable families of behavior characteristics in order to ensure usefulness when used in conjunction with other components. The more that narrowly focused system characteristics are enforced, the more reliable, predictable, powerful, and broad the range of applications. Modularity comes from standardization of the separate components.

Figure 18 USB standard connector

Human beings share some qualities in common; on the other hand, they are unique, and it is important that their individuality be acknowledged, accounted for, and celebrated. No two people are the same. People can flourish only when their uniqueness is acknowledged.

Talk to anyone who works closely with people every day, and they will tell you that every person they work with is in some sense unique. I have taught college for many years, and I've never had two students who were the same. In spite of the labels we use to type people (introverted, impulsive, artistic, cold, etc.), the person behind our label can still behave in an unpredictable way.

When Newton studied the force of attraction between two bodies, he treated these bodies as point masses having only primary qualities like mass, position, velocity, and acceleration. He simultaneously ignored their secondary qualities, such as color, shape, texture, chemical composition, emotional associations, and so on. It was this simplification that allowed him to come up with his famous laws of force and motion. Our technical training has conditioned us to abstract a problem by removing all secondary qualities from consideration in order to simplify analysis. In contrast to this, when dealing with human realities, it is important to give full credit to the specific, the unique, since that is where we all live our everyday lives. To say that Joe is a white upper-class middle-age Protestant heterosexual male from New York does not mean that I know all about Joe or that I can make predictions about his behavior. Joe is still a mystery I can discern only bits at a time through dialogue and empathy.

In the human terrain, universal principles only take us so far; specifics are of the essence! Don't try to abstract specifics away. Pay attention to them. It helps to stay open to surprise and mystery when dealing with other people at close range. That mind-set is also needed in our search for self-knowledge.

Escapism, Workaholism

Science presents us with a beautiful scene of order, control, and predictability. Software is an extreme example of working in an abstract universe in which all events have predictable, manmade outcomes. Especially in the computer software area, work can become an escape from the grungy, fuzzy, diffuse, self-contradicting, messy, paradoxical, constantly changing demands of the real world of human relations at home. I personally know engineers who prolong their work hours in order to stay in that orderly, predictable sub-universe provided to them by their computer monitors. Family life can be burdensome and fraught with insecurity for them.

Studies (Kidder 1981; Turkle 1984) made of workers in Santa Clara, California, also known as Silicon Valley, reveal a very competitive and stressful environment. Great commitment and excessively long hours were demanded of the workers. Divorce rates were well above the average in that region of the country. They saw an increasing alienation from families and from nature, the desire to escape human intimacy and the threat of rejection, an awareness that computers are more predictable than people.

Love

From our moment of birth, our call is to loving relatedness. This is the highest priority—perhaps the only priority—running as a thread through all our lives until our moment of death.

There is an old story of a Jewish man who dreams of a treasure buried under a bed. He decides to pursue it. He travels all over the world. After many long travels around the world, he finally comes back to his humble house. He then recognizes the bed in the dream and starts digging underneath. The treasure was buried under his bed all the time!

A thought transfixed me: for the first time in my life I saw the truth as it is set into song by so many poets, proclaimed as the final wisdom by so many thinkers. The truth—that love is the ultimate and the highest goal to which man can aspire. Then I grasped the meaning of the greatest secret that human poetry and human thought and belief have to impart: The salvation of man is through love and in love. I understood how a man who has nothing left in this world still may know bliss, be it only for a brief moment, in the contemplation of his beloved. In a position of utter desolation, when man cannot express himself in positive action, when his only achievement may consist in enduring his sufferings in the right way—an honorable way—in such a position man can, through loving contemplation of the image he carries of his beloved, achieve fulfillment (Frankl 1959).

Move to valuing people more than before. Start at home by reconnecting with your family, friends, and environment. Recognize the importance of quality relationships by seeking out and nourishing committed, close relationships that will encourage you and support you to grow. Give of yourself to others. Our quality of life is at its max when we are giving support to our loved ones and when we are open to experiencing life in all its dimensions: color, texture, music, sculpture, theater, poetry, dance.

Make a mental list of the people you routinely come in contact with. Look for telltale signs of relationships that hold you down or can be hurtful in the long term. Group pressure is an invisible, insidious force that can exert a lot of influence on us. Either move away from these people or set up conditions for yourself under which you will continue to be friends with them; don't let a group give you conditional acceptance for bad behavior. If necessary, look for and nurture new positive relationships that will encourage your growth.

"In short, the essential ingredient of successful psychotherapy is love…Intensive psychotherapy in many ways is a process of reparenting…For the most part, mental illness [barring a physical defect in the brain] is caused by an absence of or defect in the love that a particular child required from its particular parents for successful maturation and spiritual growth" (Peck 1978).

New York Times columnist David Brooks has some very insightful things to say about love:
Love does several things to reorient the soul. The first thing it does is humble us. It reminds us that we are not even in control of ourselves. In most cultures and civilizations, love is described in myth and story as an external force…that comes in and colonizes a person, refashioning everything inside…Love is like an invading army that reminds you that you are not master of your own house…Love is a surrender. You expose your deepest vulnerabilities and give up your illusions of self-mastery…

Love depends on the willingness of each person to be vulnerable and it deepens that vulnerability… "You will be loved the day when you will be able to show your weakness without the person using it to assert his strength," the Italian novelist Caesar Pavese wrote…

Next, love decenters the self. Love leads you out of your neutral state of self-love. Love makes other people more vivid to you than you are to yourself.

The person in love may think she is seeking personal happiness, but that's an illusion. She is really seeking fusion with another, and when fusion contradicts happiness, she will probably choose fusion.

Next, love infuses people with a poetic temperament.
(Brooks 2015, 170–2).

> If you can't find love, give love, and then you will find love.
> —John of the Cross

Monologue Compared to Dialogue

Science has as one of its many goals the desire to control the material world through technology. By knowing the laws of energy and matter, we can seek to force nature to do useful things for us.

> We control Nature by obeying Nature.
> —Francis Bacon

When working in technology, we are dealing with that part of nature that can be controlled by us; we can cut it, bend it, drill it, burn it, treat it chemically, connect it, and program it, consciously intending to exert dominion over it in order to achieve our desired result. Power is being exerted in the form of a monologue, a one-way relationship between us and nature.

In a monologue, I talk down to an inferior. I am in control; I am protected from what is happening; I am unchanged by being a participant. In a dialogue, on the other hand, if I value and include the other, I am now vulnerable to rejection or being forced to change. I am at risk of an unsure outcome. It is important to listen attentively throughout the dialogue and to respond by changing my actions as needed. The situation is not totally in my control when I dialogue: my preconceptions and my desired outcome are not guaranteed. It's important to be open to including the needs and special language of the other. I must remain vulnerable to being stretched, to experiencing change, and to compromising.

Anyone who has raised a teenager to adulthood will readily agree that this can be a life-transforming experience, not only for the teen, but very much so for the parent as well! It is impossible to raise children without having our vision challenged, our sacred cows upset, our peace disturbed. To raise a child requires that the boundaries of our comfort zone be sorely stretched well beyond what we think we are capable of. We never know how much we are capable of doing until our loved ones require heroic responses from us. Spirituality, likewise, is a life-transforming experience.

Compared to technology, on the other hand, religion deals with something mysterious, much greater than ourselves, outside our control. Instead of being in control, as we are with technology, we are now required to cultivate an attitude of respect, receptivity, and openness to mystery.

The spiritual use of technology requires that we first dialogue with nature and then make our decisions, including the bigger picture: both the long-term good of nature and our immediate goal. The many efforts of John Muir, Rachel Carson, and the environmental movement in general are good examples of an active dialogue between spirituality and technology.

In our technical work, we try to force a desired outcome by controlling nature.

In our spiritual search, we seek relationship with God by listening; dialoguing; staying open; and experiencing mystery, awe, and surprise.

Huston Smith has pointed out that science, because of its limited scope, can only study things that are, in some way, inferior to us.

I don't know how many times I have read the phrase "We are insignificant specks in a cold, uncaring universe." The implication is that our human size is so small compared to the solar system that we have very little value. The truth is that we are the only beings capable of forming the concept of the universe in our minds. Even though we are small in size, we are more important than all the planets put together. We are not insignificant. We have love, art, music, creativity, philosophy, and so on.

Science allows us to describe things that are inferior to us, since our minds are capable of analyzing them, and in some cases, we can control them. To connect with that which is not inferior to us requires a different mind-set and attitude.

Accepting Ambiguity and Mystery

In contrast to the clear simplicity of a mathematical equation, lived religion can be messy, diffuse, enmeshed in the grungy day-to-day lives of many cultures, dynamic, constantly changing. It has fuzzy edges; it bears the smudge of much-traveled roads throughout the ages of human history. Religion is not always above apparent self-contradictions and paradox.

Working in a technical environment brings with it a habit of constant questioning. It likewise takes determination to live in a state of some amount of perennial ambiguity in our spiritual struggles. Faith in the process, faith in a final result, is required in both cases.

> Faith is not certainty. It is the courage to live
> with uncertainty. Jonathan Sacks

Spiritual progress is not always noticeable, since we humans tend to change slowly. Every so often, we will reach a milestone that surprises us with the realization that, yes, we have made some progress. We can be disappointed if we have rigid expectations that removing unknowns is just a matter of time, skill, resources, and effort. It helps if we can stay constantly open to new possibilities that we may not have anticipated.

Including Our Inner World

I'm asking you to form an image of a house in your mind's eye. As you look at a house, you can only see the external part of it, the outward appearance. You notice the color, architecture, upkeep, front lawn of the house, well knowing that the real action is taking place inside, hidden from your view. Occasionally, a door or window will open, and you can get a limited peek into a part of the house.

Let's use this image of a house as a very rough metaphor for human beings. You know things about a person that are obvious; they can be seen from the outside. We will refer to this as the "outer world." Then there are parts of the person that are hidden from outside view. We occasionally get glimpses of them when a door opens momentarily. We will call this the "inner world." The inner world cannot be readily seen, yet it has tremendous energy and impact on our lives. It follows us wherever we go and affects our life choices markedly.

There is an external world around us that is obvious to our senses. This world is tangible, and we use our common sense to operate in it. Science gives us tools to predict and control the behavior of material objects in this external world.

There is also an internal world, a whole universe inside each one of us. This internal world has been acknowledged and valued for thousands of years in cultures all around the globe. Some cultures actually hold the inner world to be more real than the outer world.

Whether we like it or not, our inner world has a major impact on who we are, how we perceive things, and how we respond to them. This inner world is pretty much out of the reach of number-based physical science. It has very tangible effects on us, yet science cannot measure it quantitatively or tell us how to control it.

Science and technology target all their energies toward achieving a goal in the outer world. Spirituality, on the other hand, operates in two realms simultaneously: both the inner and the outer worlds.

In the outer world, we can make a difference in our surroundings and in our relationships with our coworkers, our family, our relatives, and our friends. We are also called to bring about social change to help the needy or marginalized people of the world.

Our inner world contains traces of all our lived life experiences, our emotions, our imagination and creativity, our connection to the larger universe. Much of our energy and inspiration comes from our inner world. Our inner world is hidden, but it contains very powerful parts of ourselves, calling for our attention.

Another model that can help us visualize the inner world of human beings consists of visualizing a beautiful core with things around it. The central core contains the image of God (*imago Dei*), with all God's love, goodness, spontaneity, rationality, creativity, joy, openness. This central core is surrounded by vestiges of our past life experiences, limited experiences, hurtful occasions, rejections, faulty self-image, self-defeating behavior, the undeveloped parts of us. Healing and opening up the outer layers so that our inner core can shine out will help us blossom and become fully alive children of God.

Open Ended, Open to Mystery and Surprise

When working on a technical research or production project, we get used to pursuing a sharply defined goal with a great amount of focus and energy. We are operating under expected outcomes and schedules. On the other hand, when struggling with our spiritual development, it helps to stay open since we cannot take in a view of the total scope of our undertakings. We can't schedule or plan rigidly. We are not in total control; openness and receptivity are now asked of us.

We can choose to establish a structure for our spiritual development. It helps to set a goal of doing spiritual reading every day, to set time aside for prayer, to meet with spiritual friends, to deepen our sensitivity to the needs of others, to do acts of mercy to others on an ongoing basis. It is important to consciously provide some structure to our spiritual lives, so things don't just slide away from us in spite of all our good intentions.

Even though we can attempt to structure our spiritual lives, the outcomes cannot be predicted. When we pursue a technical objective, we anticipate and work toward the goal while following a schedule. In the spiritual life, the outcome often comes in the form of surprise since our lives are full of basic messiness and loose ends.

We have to work hard moving forward while remaining open to surprise. This is referred to as passionate indifference.

Self-Discovery

It is helpful to visualize our spiritual struggles as journeys. Our spiritual journeys do not follow straight-line path; they can stall or do loops, swirls, or reversals, sometimes not seeming to change at all, at other times leaving us giddy and breathless. As we grow in self-knowledge, we may become aware of weaknesses and blind spots we didn't even know we had.

Self-discovery is a process of getting to know a stranger, the stranger within us. It is a paradox that the more intimately we know our specific, unique selves, which are grounded in our personal life histories, the closer we come to knowing the universal man/woman. The universal and the unique are strangely the same. Self-knowledge challenges us to love and accept that person we find within us. In learning to accept and love my real me, I can then grow in compassion for others.

Some steps to take:

- Review your life history.
- Learn to recognize your emotions, your subconscious, and your feminine side.
- Work consciously on bringing the less developed side of you further ahead toward the well-developed side of your science training.
- Review your present state by comparing it to the works of Fowler, Maslow, and Gardner.
- Reconnect with being in your body. Years of study that emphasizes the mind as the only value and priority can

leave us disconnected from our bodies. When we spend long hours in study or research, we learn to turn off the signals from our bodies. Our bodies have been valued as if they were carts that carry our brains around. Carrying out a good dialogue with our bodies can be of great help to us. Our bodies give us signals when we are feeling an emotion. Our bodies are part of the whole of us; they can be valuable guides in solving problems.

Unexpected people, resources, and opportunities will pop up seemingly out of nowhere. We discover hidden parts of ourselves rising out from within us. We slowly become aware that our self-knowledge and planning are not the iceberg after all, but barely the tip.

Some Important Personal Issues

- Meaning vs. despair
- Self-love vs. self-destruction
- Loving relatedness vs. self-centered isolation
- Growth vs. stagnation
- Creativity vs. predictability
- Forgiveness vs. seeking revenge
- Accepting challenge vs. passivity/safety/predictability
- Seeking self-knowledge vs. being in denial
- Detachment vs. engagement/commitment
- Accepting mystery and ambiguity without clinging to our need for certainty

Exercises

- Describe some aspects that make you unique.
- Describe some of your new-found strengths.
- Describe some close friends and their unique personalities.
- What beliefs do you hold independently of science? Learn to accept the personal and irrational facets of your personality.
- What values do you cherish?
- How aware are you of your inner world? Describe some aspects of it.
- How do you feel about accepting subjective truth?
- What is unique about you that you value specially? You have unique history and unique ways of reacting to things. This is who you really are! Spend time learning to love and cherish this unique, peculiar being you are.
- Is your work affecting your personal life in a negative way?
- Describe the times you have felt truly loved and the effect it has had on you.
- How did it feel when someone talked at you without including you or being aware of your feelings?
- Do you remember a time when a loved one entered into a loving dialogue with you? When you felt special and cared for? When your special needs were acknowledged and valued?

For Further Reading

O'Connor, Peter. 1985. *Understanding Jung, Understanding Yourself.* New York: Paulist Press.

Rogers, Carl. 1961. *On Becoming a Person: A Therapist's View of Psychotherapy.* New York: Houghton Mifflin.

Chapter 9
A Treasury of Spiritual Practices

Because the things in the world
are mutable and corruptible,
it is necessary they should have an author.
Because they are arranged in a rational way
and in a very beautiful order,
it is necessary that they should have been
created
in accordance with wisdom.
But, because the Creator, rationally
speaking,
is in need of nothing,
having perfection and sufficiency in himself,
it is necessary that he should create
what he does create
through benevolence and love.
—William of St. Thierry
(Dronke 1988, 367)

Preview

Being religious is not automatically a sign of softness, infantile irrationality, lack of courage, provincialism, or tunnel vision. Religion is not a mental sickness or weakness; it is a natural, deep part of all humans, regardless of place or historical period. As we survey world history, we find that from the very beginning, a multitude of the greatest accomplishments have been motivated by spiritual aspirations: magnificent temples, pyramids, petroglyphs, pottery, paintings, sculpture, dance, jewelry, body ornamentation, music, literature, philosophical thought, and so on. Humans throughout the ages have felt a need to express their relation to the divine as perceived by their culture. Keep in mind that different cultures in different eras will use a variety of metaphors and symbols to express their personal experiences of the divine, creating a beautiful, expansive kaleidoscope of forms and expressions that can fill us with awe!

To experience what artists have tried to communicate to us about their spiritual feeling, visit a temple. Give yourself time to absorb the size, the height, the sense of awe. Try to say, in words, some of the things that the building and its artwork evoke in you.

We know of no people anywhere on the face of the earth who, at any time over the past 100,000 years have been without religion...In the nineteenth century the European intellectual tradition gave rise to the idea that science would ultimately destroy religion by showing people the irrationality of their myths and rituals. Indeed, the belief is still widespread that as scientific explanations replace those of religion, the latter should wither on the vine. An opposite tendency has occurred...
The persistence of religion in the face of Western rationalism clearly reveals that it is a powerful and dynamic force in society (Haviland 1987, 311).

A study of world art history from prehistoric times to our times is like watching a multicolored parade of rich, multifaceted manifestations of the human spirit. We can truly say that if you could somehow magically make all spiritually inspired works disappear, there would not be much left of human thought and art.

Religion is not some pure ethereal abstraction written on a lofty document somewhere. It is organic; dynamic; ever changing; a lived experience with all the grungy day-to-day growing pains, blind spots, and contradictions that a living culture normally experiences. At times, religion is too structured and can be criticized for that. Religion can at times experience inertia, which makes change slow and painful. At other times, religion can become too loose and hard to pin down. Religious expressions are organic, so they have changed throughout the centuries, adapting to new environments and new perspectives.

Prayer on the Run

Good news! The desire to pray is itself prayer!

We have already discussed the all-pervasive presence of the divine mind throughout the universe. A very simple and flexible spiritual practice consists of being consciously, lovingly aware of God's presence all day long as you run through your mundane daily life activities. God is everywhere, not only in awe-inspiring cathedrals or stunningly beautiful natural settings. God cares for you and is accessible wherever you are.

Awaken and deepen your sense of constant thankfulness to God for all you have received. A thankful heart is a foundation for all spirituality.

Were you ever fortunate enough to have someone you felt totally accepted by just as you were then and with whom you felt you could truly be yourself? You can use this same setting for your daily relationship with God. Establish a safe, loving environment within yourself and within that space, share your feelings and aspirations openly with God, carrying on a conversation off and on all day long. Remain open to feeling a response. Remember that you're not writing anything down or sharing this openly with anyone else. Give yourself permission to be totally candid, truly your special, unique self. The beginning, the very essence of spirituality is a deep sense of thankfulness. Keep this sense of thankfulness always active as a foundation for your prayer.

A Spiritual Community

I can't remember the last time I saw a movie in which church members were not shown as being self-righteous, close-minded bigots. Our entertainment media has had a strong bias against the positive elements of practiced religion. Contrary to this stereotype, there are sane, intelligent, balanced people of good faith struggling to make a difference in the world by practicing their faith day by day.

It is a supreme act of self-righteousness to despair of ever finding a church "good enough for me." To grow in faith, we need to have a support community. We need to see practical spirituality lived out in a variety of ways corresponding to the different people and their life situations and unique personalities.

A Spiritual Friend

In addition to a faith community, we need to have some close friendships. A good friend will encourage us and give us suggestions and feedback while letting us be our own person. We can pray together, journal together, grow together.

Setting

Where is God? Where do I have to go to meet God? The Western world has a long tradition of building beautiful churches with great architecture and, in some cases, paintings or sculptures. The architecture and decoration of the church is meant to help us experience a sense of awe at being faced with something larger than ourselves. It is tempting to think that when we want to meet God, God is inside a building, inside of a church.

Primal societies typically have special places—rocks, groves of trees, caves, rivers, and so on—that possess a privileged sense of

God's presence. At the same time, there is also a culture that sees God everywhere, completely containing us in our everyday lives. All is sacred; nothing is left out.

We're all familiar with the Sistine Chapel paintings that show us God as an old man with a flowing white beard floating up in the sky. We are likewise tempted to seek God in a beautiful setting in nature by going to a special park or a beach with a fantastic view. There are many references in scripture to God as being up in heaven above. Keep in mind that *up* is a metaphor for a higher state of spirituality and should not always be interpreted literally.

If possible, create a place at home where you can go to pray or read without distractions. Make sure that phones, TV, and iPhones can't reach you there. If you have many unresolved issues bouncing around inside your mind, make a list of all these and leave this list outside that room so you don't forget them, but you will look at them in the future. If necessary, go for a walk or sit in your car, but it's important that you have a space where you will not be disturbed. You can enhance your prayer space by putting up objects that have special meaning to you: pictures of loved ones, pictures of beautiful nature settings, flowers, seashells, driftwood, pictures of some of your heroes, and so on. Find a comfortable posture. If you have problems with falling asleep, sit forward in the chair so your back does not rest against the chair's back; this will help you to stay awake. If nothing works, you probably need a nap; take it. When at work, I have sometimes left the building to walk around the block or sit in my car in the parking lot in order to find a quiet space.

You can begin your prayer time by closing your eyes and softly slowing down your breath while repeating a mantra or short prayer phrase. Scan your body for tight spots and release those muscles. If you have problems with severe muscle tension, take each muscle in your body one at a time, slowly tense it, then release it very slowly. Keep repeating this tense/release sequence until that muscle lets go of its tension.

Always be selective in what you read. Be aware of the author's credentials. Avoid sensationalism and shallow entertainment. Read slowly without rushing to get to the end. Monitor yourself as you read, looking for your own reactions.

In our teens, when we first became infatuated with someone else, we dove in, expecting an unending experience of bliss and union. As we became more and more involved with that other person, we discovered that we had actually opened ourselves up to a whole wide panorama of wrenching emotions that can stretch us beyond our comfort zones. Likewise, any of our emotions can become energized during prayer—not just the pleasant ones, but all of them, none excluded! The push and the pull, the peaks and the valleys, the insights and the blind spots, the high points and the lows, the breakthroughs and the drudgery, the sense of comfort and the fear of abandonment, our dazzling insights and our being muddle brained, all can take place during our prayer.

Spiritual Paths (Temperament)

When we decide to take on a spiritual path, it is common to want to imitate somebody we know and admire. This may be someone in our family, a figure from history, a religious leader or minister. Before we set out to imitate people, it's important to have some self-knowledge. There are many different spiritual paths that we can follow. Trying to fit into the wrong path can be a source of frustration (Phillips 1952).

"There is no such thing as a good hand-me-down religion. To be vital, to be the best of which we are capable, our religion must be a wholly personal one, forged entirely through the fire of our questioning and doubting in the crucible of our experience and reality" (Peck 1978, 194).

Let's review some of the factors that influence choice of spiritual paths. You may find this hard to believe, but much work has been done in determining what prayer styles "work" for different people. We will now break people into four groups of pairs having opposite orientations. For more detail, see Keirsey (Keirsey and Bates 1984), Francis (Francis and Robbins 2008, 67–84), and Michael (Michael and Norrisey 1984). This material is not meant to be rigid and "all or nothing"; it is mean to give us guidelines only. Most of us are mixtures of these opposite orientations, placing a strong dependence on one and less on the other.

Some polarities in people's temperaments:

— Alone...or...with others
— Intuition...or...senses
— Thinking...or...feeling
— Orderly...or...spontaneous

Four Pairs of Opposites

1. People who are energized by interacting with others versus people energized by being by themselves

Picture two people going to a party. After the party is over, one will go home refreshed, energized, fulfilled; the other person will go home tired, seeking renewal, needing to be by him- or herself. Review your own history of interacting with others and decide which of these two responses describes you best. Factor this insight about yourself into your choice of a spiritual path.

If you find yourself energized by interacting with people, you want to include group activities as a priority in your spiritual practices (charitable or church group activities, public prayer, a leadership position, community work, social activism, mentoring or counseling others, being a spiritual friend or companion to someone).

If, on the other hand, you find yourself energized by being by yourself, you want to include private activities as a priority in your spiritual practices instead (reading, meditating, listening to music, private prayer, nature walks, journaling).

2. People who base their knowledge of the world on use of their senses (physical setting, sound, taste, color, texture, room temperature, facial expressions, dress) versus those who predominantly use their intuition and imagination (by seeing future potential)

Picture two people riding in a car past an abandoned empty lot surrounded by tall, attractive office buildings. One person will capture in great detail all the physical appearance of the lot while the other will envision the future potential of developing that empty lot.

When a sensing person goes into a room, he or she immediately notices the lighting, colors, textures, placement of objects, people's postures, the expressions on their faces, and so on. They focus on the details of the here and now; they value tangible experience: "Seeing is believing" or "Show me." If this sounds like you, make it a priority, whenever possible, to include hands-on, tangible activities as part of your prayer: charitable work, arts and crafts, drawing, painting, clay modeling, cooking, drawing, carpentry, playing music, dancing, hiking, gardening. Also consider praying with your whole body through interpretive dance movements, by which you express your feelings and intentions through the use of body posture and motions.

When an intuitive person walks into the same room, he or she perceives the mood of the room, what has happened previously that leads to the present moment, and the potential of what is taking place in the room. Intuitive people like to use their imaginations and inspirations, following future-oriented motivation. If this sounds like you, make it a priority to allow your intuition to take an active

211

part during your prayer time. Read from a book and then let the implications of what you just read develop in your mind.

3. People who rely on objective logic to reach conclusions versus those who rely on subjective appreciation of the personal and interpersonal factors involved

When a thinking person is faced with a problem to solve, he or she will strive to work for the objective truth. Our technical training emphasizes this mode almost exclusively.

If this sounds like you, be sure to include your reasoning powers as tools to gain a deeper understanding of what you read during your prayer time. Read scholarly works on spirituality or science. You can give of your time to solve technical problems for the community or tutor needy students.

When a feeling person is faced with a problem to solve, he or she relies on subjective appreciation of the personal and interpersonal factors involved. If this sounds like you, be sure to include the use of empathy and feelings to deepen your participation in your prayer meditations. Actively show compassion for those who are needy or hurting.

4. Orderly people versus spontaneous people

Some people naturally gravitate toward orderliness, while others are more naturally spontaneous.

If you are naturally organized, scheduled, and planned, you will find it helpful and natural to include some schedule, structure, and order in your prayer activities.

If you tend to be flexible, spontaneous, and unplanned, be sure to give yourself permission to include spontaneous, unstructured activities in your prayer. Respond to your feelings in prayer.

Benedictine Prayer

It is very helpful to establish a habit of doing a short spiritual reading every day. A very good technique for doing this is what is called Benedictine Prayer. (See Dysinger and Paintner 2011). This form of prayer has been used for thousands of years and was initiated into the Christian tradition by Saint Benedict, who started Western monasticism. It's extremely simple; it has just four well-defined parts that are very easy to understand and follow. These parts need not be followed in any specific order. I will present them to you sequentially, but you can actually move back and forth then circle around and go back and repeat a part as wanted.

Setting: Find a safe, comfortable place free of distractions. Quiet your body and your mind. You can let go of body tension and distractions by slowing down your breathing while rhythmically repeating a short prayer phrase or mantra. You can have your journal by your side to write down your experience, the insights you receive, and any resolves for the future.

Working material: Select a short reading. This reading may come from scripture, an inspirational writing, a poem, a personal letter, or your personal journal. You can use any material that has special meaning to you. Do not set a goal of covering a certain amount of material by some schedule. Less is better! Slow is better!

1. **Read:** Very s-l-o-w-l-y read your chosen material, taking in the feeling, the tone, the symbols used, and the evolving themes of the text. As you do this, you will find that at some point a response is welling up within you, coming to the surface, a blip on the radar. Stay with this feeling. Stay in a passive and receptive mode with this emotion-laden response, and let it fill you for a while.

2. **Meditate:** Take this special word, passage, or image and gently repeat it to yourself over and over again with great

reverence. Allow it to interact with your thoughts, hopes, memories, and desires.

3. **Express your response in words:** Moving on to the third part, which consists of spoken prayer, verbalize your reaction to the reading after meditating on it, and speak to God, expressing in words your insights, needs, and reactions or any new changes within you. Stay sensitive and open to any sense of a response. You can write these things down in your journal if you want to.

   You may at times need to return to reading the original text again literally in order to deepen your understanding of the reading. Keep cycling around these stages as long as needed.

4. **Wordless "sitting with":** In contemplation, let go of words, sit quietly, just lovingly paying attention to what is happening inside you. That is, you let go of control, of analysis, of words. Simply be still, open, and attentive to what you may receive.

   Contemplative (wordless) prayer has been used for thousands of years. It goes beyond the limitations of words. Our vocabulary of known words is limited, so when we try to use words all the time for prayer, we limit what can be included. Silence goes beyond words; it is more general. If you reflect on the strongest moments of your life, you will most probably find yourself saying "I was just left speechless!"

   In contemplation, we go beyond words. We just sit quietly while God interacts with us without words.

   This prayer is centered on scripture, but it doesn't have to be. You can choose a poem that you like, a song that touches your heart, an old love letter, or a faded photograph of an event. The experience of going through old letters, photos, and memorabilia can have great energy, bringing out powerful, life-transforming energy from mere faded scraps of paper. There is a song called "Traces" that expresses very beautifully the evocative power of remembering.

Using Imagination in Prayer

One way to think of prayer is as a conversation in which we verbalize our thoughts or feelings, our aspirations, and our disappointments. There is also a very powerful way of praying in which we use our imaginations in order to enter into the scene being meditated upon and experience it more vividly.

You take an action narrative from scripture, from a letter, from a story, or from an important event in your past. You first read the narrative in order to build a sense of place. Visualize the setting with all its sensations: the feeling tone, the smells, sounds, and so on. Create a visual picture of each one of the participants: their appearances, roles, and personalities. After you've read the story slowly one or more times, using your imagination, allow yourself to enter into the story as a witness who is completely surrounded by the sights and sounds of the narrative setting. Rerun the action narrative slowly, staying alert and sensitive to all that is taking place. When you finish your meditation, return to the world around you and spend some time writing down all your experiences and insights in your journal.

Journaling

(This section was contributed by Barbara Manseau Hamer.)

215

Journaling is a simple but powerful tool; it can be used to process and find the meaning contained in your past experiences, as a tool for growth in self-knowledge, or as an anchor that allows you to weather the great storms of life (Kelsey 1980).

Journaling, like all good things in this world, takes a decision on your part. When you decide to start writing down your thoughts, choose a time when you are alert. Set yourself down in a quiet place, a place where hopefully you'll have no interruptions. Have paper and pencil or your electronic writing device with you. Set yourself up with what you need.

Let your thoughts come as they will. Don't censor them. Let the words appear on the paper as they come into your mind. Let this stream of consciousness happen.

Perhaps you want to write about an experience you encountered. Write it out. Let your emotions enter into your writing. Don't judge your words, sentence structure, or punctuation.

Perhaps you want to write about your feelings. Let them all hang out. Feel free with your feelings.

Perhaps you want to use your journaling time as your prayer time. Open a daily meditation guide, the Bible, a prayer book, or some other spiritual guide. Read the daily entry, find a scripture passage, or choose a sentence or two in the prayer book or guide. Dwell on some of the words and/or phrases, allowing them to speak to you. This may help you get started. Do the words bring to mind something within you that you've been concerned about, something that has been troubling you? Is anger, grief, or a troubled heart coming into your conscious state? Talk to God in your writing. Be honest with your feelings. God can take anything you want to say to Him. Write it all out.

Or perhaps you relate to a passage in an upbeat way. You find yourself praising God, thanking Him for all the ways He has blessed you. Write down your praises, your thanksgivings. There are many different scripture passages in the Bible that can elicit all kinds of emotions. Look around the Old and New Testaments. I've found Isaiah and the Psalms in the Old Testament and the writings of Paul in the New Testament to be helpful through the years. The accounts of what went on in those times with their stories and prayers are relevant in today's world. They are there to help you. It has been said that the Bible is God's love letter to us. Read it. Let your inner self relate to it.

Things may come up that you are not even aware are in you! Just let them flow out of you. You may surprise yourself with what you write down. Honor it. Let it be.

Of course, there may be days when nothing arises from inside you, days when you just sit there and look at the blank paper or screen. Don't be discouraged. Not every day will be like that. Every day is a new day with a new beginning.

When you are able to write, don't be nervous about seeing your thoughts in black and white. You can always destroy this writing after you've finished. You don't have to keep it if you don't want to. But the writing will sometimes help release the negative energy that's been stored up within you. It pushes that energy out of you where it can't possess you anymore. The writing may also release positive energy that will relax you, make you smile, energize you, and help heal you.

You may find that you enjoy this encounter with yourself. You may find yourself seeking and finding the time during the day to write down your thoughts. If possible, try to journal at the same time every day. Give yourself time to meet yourself and the God within you.

Remember, your journal writings are private. You don't have to share them with anyone if you don't want to. They came from you, and they stay with you.

May journaling become a lifelong habit. It's something simple and positive that you can do for yourself. Try it! You may like journaling as a spiritual practice!

Discernment

When you feel you have received something from your inner world, such as an image, a phrase, an insight, or a conviction of some kind, you always have to go one step further. Take your present understanding and weigh it carefully. You should never be asked to hurt another person or yourself in any way. Nothing should result from your inner conversation that would violate the teachings of scripture. When in doubt, talk to someone you trust before you go any further. You never act as a passive person, simply taking dictation and following that blindly; you always should use common sense and discretion. If still in doubt, wait or do nothing.

Remember that not all use of language is meant to be literal. Be alert to when language is being used in suggestive, metaphorical, or symbolic ways. There was an incident reported in the newspapers some years ago when a woman turned on the garden hose in her backyard and let it run full blast. Three weeks went by, and her yard was flooded, as were her neighbors' yards. The police were called, and she was finally forced to turn off the water. She said she had heard voices that told her to turn on the water; she took this literally. If I had heard that, I would interpret "turning on the water" as being a symbol of needing to attend to or care for the garden of my soul. Literalism can give hurtful outcomes at times; it can also give a person an inflated sense of self-importance, of being a direct conduit of God's word; no talking back allowed.

Finding God in Nature

Make it a priority to have contact with nature in your everyday life. Notice plants and the vegetables you are eating; notice trees, clouds, variations in sunlight, changes in the weather. Consciously become aware of the cycle of the seasons. Pick up leaves, pebbles, driftwood. Look at textures, variations in the coloration of all organic things around you. Make it a point to have the presence of nature at your work desk; bring in small objects or growing plants to your work area. Plant a seed in a glass of water and watch it grow. When we mindfully observe organic growth in front of us, we're watching an incredible ballet, full of grace and beauty: God acting through nature with great beauty, with incredible sophistication of engineering and survival skills.

Browse through an anatomy and physiology textbook. Look at artist renditions of the inner world of a cell. Sensitize yourself to the exquisite and elaborate mathematical patterns that are to be found in Nature all around and within us (Huntley 1970; Skinner, 2006). Actively acknowledge, cherish, and nurture your childlike sense of wonder!

Finding God within Yourself

Review your life history. Recall the hard times; recall the times when you were able to survive despite overwhelming odds. You will see that there is a great spirit acting within you that gives you the strength to be, the will to live, the creativity to solve problems, the ingenuity to survive. Learn to know yourself, accept yourself, cherish yourself. You are one of God's unique great creations, God's handiwork!

Take some time to review your past life for self-knowledge: think of your childhood, your early family life, your technical studies, your career and family. Write down a brief description of important events in your life and the environments in which you lived. Make a list of your survival skills, strengths, and unique talents. Likewise, make a list of personal factors that have held you back.

219

Create a profile of yourself and of the environments in which you have lived. Identify strengths and weaknesses, opportunities and barriers.

Finding God in Others

We live in a rushed environment, where being listened to is a rarity. "Fact and run" communication is king! Despite all this, God is present in all the people around you. Covering the huge variety of personalities and life stories, God is there. We can intuit or experience God when we develop our ability to carry on I-thou relations with others. (See the chapter on interpersonal relations.) (Buber 1937). Make it a point to get to know the people around you: people at work, in your neighborhood, at your church, in your club activities. Make it a habit to read the lives of famous people across the ages (Schmidt 2008). Observe spirituality operating in a wide variety of settings and challenges. As you get to hear people's stories you will see how God has acted in their lives to let them survive difficult times and still thrive within their own backgrounds.

Hurts

Make a list of people who have hurt you or held you back in life. Accept their limitations, and work on forgiving them. Forgiveness is easier to talk about than it is to carry out. Forgiving others can take time and concentrated efforts on your part. When we don't forgive, we carry around a burden of negative energy, a load that limits us and drains our energy and can literally poison our outlook on life.

Make a list of people you have hurt or held back in their development. Spend time trying to feel what they must have felt. Strive to grow in your self-knowledge from this experience and sensitize yourself in order to avoid having this happen again. Seek forgiveness for hurting others, and if possible, try to make amends.

Giving of Yourself

Make it a conscious practice to go out of your way to listen to people. Take time to listen attentively, taking in details and savoring them, appreciating the insights you then gain about the other person. As you open yourself up to listening to people, you will see a great reservoir of beauty and survivor's strength emanating from them, and they might likewise open up to listen to you.

Become aware of people's needs and respond to these as best you can. The very first need we all have is the need to be recognized, to know that somebody listens to us, is attentive to us, and acknowledges our uniqueness. Become involved with the people around you and respond to their needs.

An important and natural arena for our spirituality resides in our daily professional work: doing our daily tasks with dedication and honesty.

> I don't know who—or what—put the question. I don't know when it was put. I don't even remember answering. But at some moment I did answer Yes to Someone—or Something—and from that hour I was certain that existence is meaningful and that therefore, my life, in self-surrender, had a goal.
>
> —Dag Hammarskjold
> Nobel Peace Prize winner
> Secretary-General of the United Nations

Mantras

When you are reading, a particular phrase may have a special meaning for you: your radar suddenly shows a blip. That blip, that resonance you experience coming from that word or phrase is inviting you to go in even deeper. One way you can enter more deeply into a word is to turn it into a mantra. A mantra is a short prayer phrase or exclamation that you repeat in synchrony with your breath. A mantra may be prayed silently or out loud and can be used during your private prayer time or repeated silently throughout the course of your day.

Words can carry a boundless amount of energy within them. Think of a simple word, the word *yes*. Think back in your long, circuitous life journey to when you came to a fork in the road and you said yes instead of no to life. That *yes* is asking to be acknowledged, celebrated, and absorbed more intensely into your depths, so it becomes a powerful long-lasting beacon of light for you!

Choose a phrase that carries a special energy for you. Carry this phrase with you throughout the day, and keep repeating it in rhythm with your breath. As you repeat this phrase, its energy penetrates more and more deeply into your being; you are internalizing the deep meaning of the mantra. You can get a mantra from a short scripture quote, from a poem, from a love letter.

Try repeating the word *yes* or *forward* or *recover* or the short phrase *I am at home* or *I am loved* in synchrony with your breath over and over for an indefinite amount of time, and you will see that this can make a difference in your life. Repeating a prayer phrase with your breath can counter negative emotions that threaten to engulf you, such as fear, anxiety, or anger.

Mantras and Prayer Phrases

Here are a few selections from book of Psalms:

Ps 2: "Happy are those who take shelter in him."

Ps 4: "Lord, you've given more joy to my heart than others ever knew (for all the corn and wine)."

"In peace I lie down, and fall asleep at once, since you alone, Lord, make me rest secure."

Ps 5: "I say this prayer to you, Lord, for at daybreak you listen for my voice; and at dawn I hold myself in readiness for you, I watch for you."

"But I, so great is your love, may come to your house."

"But joy for all who take shelter in you, endless shouts of joy!"

"Since you protect them, they exult in you, those who love your name."

Ps 8: "Yahweh, our Lord, how great your name throughout the earth! Above the heavens is your Majesty chanted by the mouths of children, babes in arms. I look up at your heavens, made by your fingers, at the moon and stars you set in place—ah, what is man that you should spare a thought for him, the son of man that you should care for him? Did you have made him little less than the God, your crowned with glory and splendor, made them Lord or the works of your hands, several things under his feet. Yahweh, our Lord, how great your name throughout the earth!"

Ps 18: "In my distress I called to the Lord And to my God I cried; from his temple he heard my voice, my cry came to his ears."

"Lord, you yourself are my lamp, my God lights up my darkness."

Ps 19: "The heavens declare the glory of God, the vault of heaven proclaims his handiwork; day discourses of it today, night to night hands on the knowledge."

Ps 84: "Even the sparrow finds a home, And the swallow a nest in which she puts her young."

Figure 19 Carl Jung

Our Shadow

Psychologist Carl Jung (Jung et al. 1964; O'Connor 1985) gave therapy to people over many decades. He noticed a recurrent pattern. Human beings do not develop all their inborn capabilities at once; they do it gradually in two main stages. In the first half of life, we tend to develop half our potentiality. At this point, we are out of balance; this is the price we pay for early entry into life's arena. In the second half of life, we gradually become aware of our undeveloped side and begin working on its development. This uncomfortable process typically begins sometime in midlife.

Our developed side is quite obvious to us. It has produced our visible accomplishments and successes, our functionality, our productivity. Our undeveloped side consists of the parts of us that are weak, incomplete, or totally missing. We have blind spots that can be obvious to people around us but not to us. Our undeveloped side holds us back in life and, in some cases, can be quite hurtful to us and to the people around us.

An important part of our spiritual path consists of becoming aware of our undeveloped side and helping it grow. To be fully alive, we need to have our undeveloped side worked on. We likewise need to be aware of our dark, sometimes destructive, self-limiting side, so we can stay on guard!

- If our training and work experience have been predominantly masculine projects, our feminine side can be underdeveloped, and vice-versa.
- If our training was predominantly logical/analytical, our intuitive and relational side can be undeveloped.
- If we have been taught to read denotation only, our awareness of the emotional connotation content of communication might need some more attention.
- If our education and our accomplishments in our profession have made us feel superior to other people, it is important to work on our awareness and appreciation of the worth of other people's talents that are different from our own.
- If the goal of our professional work has been the control and power over nature through technology, our respect for nature and our ability to have dialogue and to give service to others may have been neglected.
- If our education has totally bypassed issues of meaning, our deep need for meaning in life will have been neglected, leaving a void in our lives that can lead to long-term habitual depression.
- If our professional education and work bypassed the consideration of ethical issues, it becomes important to sensitize ourselves to the potential good or evil

consequences of our work. How does my work affect humanity, for better or for worse?

— If we use technical language exclusively at work, it will be helpful to work on consciously broadening our use of language that also includes other areas, such as feeling, relationship, caring, art, and literature.

Self-Knowledge

In science and technology, we are used to all our energies and attention having a predominant focus on something that is happening outside us: an experiment on the lab bench, an electrical measurement, a schedule, a software program, the construction of a system, a test result, production yields, and so on. Something happens in the outside world, and we need to react to this.

Our spirituality will very strongly center on our own peculiar personalities, life experiences, self-images, and settings in life. We will be called to spend a lot more of our time struggling with self-knowledge, acknowledging our limitations, eliciting our strengths, reviewing our past, modifying our self-image, and healing our past hurts. Our unique, subjective selves are of paramount importance.

Chapter 10
Personal Reflections

Passion! The central theme of this book is passion, a passion to live life to its fullest! We daily receive the incredible and sacred gift of life, one heartbeat at a time. Even though the tools of science are powerful for dealing numerically with matter and energy, yet we need to look elsewhere when pursuing our other essential human needs (Maslow): self-esteem, belongingness and love, affection, meaning, beauty, self-actualization, spirituality, and transcendence.

Gift! All is gift! Our daily life is full of sacred events, some so mundane that they quietly pass unnoticed by us, some life-changing and memorable. We can respond to gifts received by returning our gratitude and love. Thankfulness is the very foundation of prayer.

The sense of wonder came naturally to us as children, but in the process of growing up, this gift may have diminished in us. I now believe that nothing is really trivial, unworthy of our attention. I have learned to think small, think every-day, think simple. I invite you to join me as I vow to myself to refresh my childlike curiosity and strive to live a grateful, wonder-full life every day!

A positive self-image is essential for our mental health. Attempting to use machine-like concepts of matter and energy to provide us with complete models for human beings can dehumanize us and can set a brick wall to our personal self-valuing and potential growth. It is important to keep in mind that we are free to exercise our freedom, spontaneity, and creativity.

We have ahead of us a challenging lifelong search for self-knowledge, working towards being able to know, accept and love our unique, subjective self. Our emotions can be guides in this search. I am constantly asking myself throughout my day as I interact with people and situations: "What emotion am I feeling right now? What is it trying to tell me?" As we discover things about ourselves which we like, as well as things that we don't like, we can learn to also be more accepting of other people's shortcomings

We can review our past lives by keeping a spiritual journal as a tool for getting to better know our unique self. We can use journaling to process our special life events, our "Aha!" moments, our eye-openers, our received blessings. Just as importantly, we can use journaling to post-process our hurts from the past so as to grow from them instead of being enslaved by them. Our past hurts, when not attended to by us, can have the power to continue hurting us and those around us.

Some years ago, when discussing religion with a wise friend, I had it pointed out to me that some of my concepts about God were still those of a child. I responded by doing reading on my own plus attending retreats and taking classes. When one has not participated in religious practices since being very young, our limited early child-like conceptions of God can hold us back when facing more complex real-life adult problems. I have spent time reviewing my childhood early life experiences of religion, both good and bad, and newly processed them as an adult in order to achieve a more experienced adult level of comprehension.

Some of the most significant events in my life have been beyond my understanding. When I reflect on my reactions to these special life events, I see mystery! As I get to know other people more closely, I experience mystery. When I look at my reflection in the mirror, I see mystery! When I reflect on my inner life, once more, I experience mystery! To be human and to experience mystery goes hand-in-hand. We can respond to mystery by becoming dogmatic, by denying its existence, or we can accept it as a fact of life. Accepting mystery can be unsettling, it questions whether we are in control or not, whether we really fully understand what is in front of us. It takes courage, openness, and faith to accept mystery as a fact of life.

Knowing that science and spirituality use language differently, and that language is normally used at an unconscious level, it helps to stay alert about possible problems in that area. Ethnocentric knee-jerk reactions can surely derail our spiritual search at an early stage. It helps to stay sensitive to going beyond the literal reading of words, listening for metaphor, connotation, story, theme, and symbol.

Science is, by all means, society's single greatest source of material power and control through the use of technology in industry as well as in the military. We science-professionals need to consciously make sure that the fruits of our work will be used in a sensitive, imaginative way to improve human life, not to hurt it. Nature is not inferior to us, available to be exploited at our whim or to satisfy our egos. The earth and all of its creatures represents our common home.

It takes openness, sensitivity, effort, and awareness of our inner world and emotions to establish a heart-to-heart relationship with another human being. Buber's I-THOU insight helps us to understand why we can feel that it's a sacred experience to really be listened to or for us to listen to the depths of another person. Listening to others involves momentarily getting out of our self-absorption in order to enter momentarily into the mindset of the other. We live in a needy, lonely, hurting world. We have some great gifts to offer others, our compassion and our loving presence.

Gardner's work in multiple intelligences can be represented by a pie chart containing 9 slices representing each intelligence. Our formal technical education can cover only a few of these slices. Cultivating an awareness of the other "slices" can help us to appreciate the rich tapestry of talents found in our human family at large. Simultaneously, this invites us to stretch ourselves in our personal growth. We are a small, but unique, and very significant, part of a larger whole which includes and values past historical periods, other countries, cultures, and disciplines.

I have pursued hard work, or "perspiration" in my technical career for years, without having a real conscious awareness of how much "inspiration" was actually contributing to my work. I now am in awe of the gift of inspiration as a present received, an act of generous love from God. Receiving this gift invites us to let go of control momentarily so we can deepen our relation with the gift-giver. I believe that creativity, a received gift common to all human disciplines, is one more gift from God, an invitation to actively participate in bringing about a better world.

The research I did for this book reintroduced me to Plato and Aristotle. I've always been in awe of them, they were truly giants! I have always loved science but now my appreciation for it has been expanded and deepened by seeing the example Copernicus, Brahe, Kepler, Galileo, and Newton set for us. I have now developed a deeper appreciation for human talents operating well outside of my historical era.

Science and religion are two valuable human endeavors, each having its own language, methods, institutions, and concerns. Occasionally, these two human endeavors "bump" into one another. Cultural differences between these two worlds can sometimes make it difficult to work in collaboration to resolve a difference. This calls for patience on our part and respect for the other side. Not all issues can be resolved in a hurry. It's OK to live with uncertainty! Patience is called for here.

Bon voyage!

Expanding My Horizons

To joyfully pursue your spiritual journey, you do not have to deny your technical self, which is such an important living part of you. The task ahead is one of reorientation, revaluing, re-visualizing, and the inclusion and valuing of new skills, not one of having to separate yourself from the excitement of being an active contributor to the field of science.

Besides speed reading work-related technical material,
I will also value slow, responsive, evocative spiritual reading.

Besides using the equation, data table, or flow chart,
I will also value the teaching story as one means of expressing the wisdom of life.

Besides reading the literal meanings of words,
I will also value metaphors and the evocative meanings of words.

Besides reading the denotation of words,
I will also value listening for personal connotations.

Besides using the equality symbol,
I will also value the proper use of metaphors.

Besides using words in prayer,
I will also value the use of silence.

Besides using my analytical intelligence,
I will also value my other intelligences (Gardner).

Besides recognizing my inherited image of God,
I will also value a modified and expanded image that matches my chronological age, my life experience, and my education.

Besides living in the present,
I will also value an awareness that I carry all my past experiences within me, and I commit to spending time processing them, looking for hidden treasures and life lessons in them.

Besides living in my outer world,
I will also value including the rich dimensions and power of my inner world.

Besides using pure reason,
I will also value my emotions, lived experience, imagination, creativity, and received inspiration.

Besides engaging in facts-only communication with others,
I will also value developing empathetic exchanges with others, looking for personal associations of words.

Besides hearing only the literal meaning of words,
I will also value being alert to finding my trigger points and their thematic connection.

Besides engaging in verbal communication,
I will also value being alert for the nonverbal parts of interpersonal communication.

Besides using monologues,

I will also value actively dialoguing with others while also listening to nature and to God.

Besides dealing in universals,
I will also value including the particulars: the uniqueness of each individual and situation.

Besides seeking knowledge, control, and power,
I will also value staying open to loving relatedness, surprise, and surrender.

Besides being concerned with the functionality of the results of my work,
I will also value being actively concerned about my work's ethical impact on humans and on the environment.

Besides engaging in scheduled, controlled activity,
I will also value developing openness and passive receptivity.

Besides my conscious, active efforts,
I will also value a sense of gratitude for inspiration received.

Besides being concerned with *how* questions,
I will also value questions of *why?*

Instead of treating a person as an *it*,
I will seek to have an I-You relationship with that person.

Metaphors

Some common metaphors:

Spatial metaphors: indicating change or decision making

Inner world/outer world

Journey, path, fork in the road, change directions

Up/down, above/below, higher/lower, raise up/bring down

In front/behind, move forward/fall back, turn around

Right/left

Near/far, closer to/move forward/turn away from, drift apart

Dead end, false start, blind alley, lost bearings

Connected to, central

Lost/found

Fall down/pick up

Some common metaphors used in spirituality

Connected to, central

Light, darkness

Heart, center, core, the cave of the heart

Open, closed

Eyes, see, open, blind, listen, deaf

Receive, embrace, reject

Father

World

Battle, warrior

Kingdom of God

Save, redeem

Some metaphors used in science

The planetary model for the atom: electrons viewed as particles orbiting around the nucleus as if they were planets.

Software platform, data bus, file folder, cloud computing, software platform, computer handshake, unlocking the secrets of the universe.

Metaphors for human struggles

The door slammed in my face; I can't run away.

Moving forward, stumbling block, hit a brick wall

I saw the light.

The father of our country

One small step for man, one giant leap for mankind

The call of a distant drummer

Turned away from my past, larger vision, getting closer

My world vision expanded.

Tied up at the office

Lifted myself up by my bootstraps, can't be moved

False idol

I lost my bearings.

In a rut, reached a fork in the road

Lost my vision

I was lifted up.

I couldn't get away from my problem.

Home base, get away from it all, hit a brick wall

Self-image, vision, the right path

Overcoming inertia, feeling scattered or lost

Disoriented, has a short fuse, reined in

Forward motivated by my surroundings

Down, up, lost

I needed to let go of childish behavior/attitude.

A closed mind

Change direction midcourse

Run away from problems

I was crushed.

Metaphors for relationships

We do not see eye to eye.

A bond started between us.

We drifted apart.

We became one.

Glass ceiling, climb the corporate ladder, inner circle, trolling

Raise the bar, below the radar, keep options open

User friendly, all tied up, good to see the light of day

A new contact, networking, World Wide Web
Below the radar

Peer group pressure

I was in the dark about the new reorganization.

My self-defensiveness boxed me in.

References

Andrews, Robert. 1993. *Columbia Dictionary of Quotations.* New York: Columbia University Press.

Antonovsky, Aaron. 1995. "The Moral and the Healthy: Identical, Overlapping, or Orthogonal?" *Israel Journal of Psychiatry and Related Sciences* 32(1).

Antonovsky, Aaron. 1987. *Unraveling the Mystery of Health: How People Manage Stress and Stay Well.* San Francisco: Jossey-Bass Publishers.

Bartlett, John, and Geoffrey O'Brien. 2002. *Bartlett's Familiar Quotations.* New York: Little, Brown and Company.

Bacon, Francis. 1267. *Opus Majus.*

Barbour, Ian G. 1993. *Ethics in an Age of Technology: The Gifford Lectures, Volume 2.* New York: Harper San Francisco.

Barbour, Ian G. 1990. *Religion and Science: Historical and Contemporary Issues.* San Francisco: Harper One.

Bellah, Robert. 1970. *Beyond Belief: Essays on Religion in a Post-Traditionalist World.* Los Angeles: University of California Press.

Blackburn, Simon. 1994. *Oxford Dictionary of Philosophy.* Oxford, England: Oxford University Press.

Bradberry, Travis, and Jean Greaves. 2003. *The Emotional Intelligence Quick Book: Everything You Need to Know to Put Your EQ to Work.* New York: Fireside.

Brewster, David. 1855. *Memoirs of the Life, Writings, and Discoveries of Sir Isaac Newton: Volume 2.* Edinburgh: Thomas Constable and Co.

Brooks, David. 2015. *The Road to Character.* New York: Random House.

Buber, Martin. 1937. *I and Thou.* New York: Charles Scribner's Sons.

Carson, Rachel. 1965. *The Sense of Wonder.* New York: Harper and Row Publishers.

Donne, John. 1987. *Devotions upon Emergent Occasions.* Edited by Anthony Respa. Quebec: McGill-Queen's University Press.

Dronke, Peter, ed. 1988. *A History of Twelfth-Century Western Philosophy*, "Thierry of Chartres", Cambridge University Press.

Dysinger, Luke O. S. B. "Lectio Divina." www.saintandrewsabbey.com.

Ecklund, Elaine Howard. 2010. *Science vs. Religion: What Scientists Really Think.* New York: Oxford University Press.

Einstein, Albert, and Leopold Infeld. 1938. *The Evolution of Physics: From Early Concepts to Relativity and Quanta.* New York: Simon and Schuster.

Ellis, Albert. 2004 *Rational Emotive Behavior Therapy: It Works for Me—It Can Work for You.* Amherst, NY: Prometheus Books.

Ferguson, Kitty. 2002. *Tycho and Kepler: The Unlikely Partnership That Forever Changed Our Understanding of the Heavens*. New York: Walker and Company.

Fowler, James. 1981. *Stages of Faith: The Psychology of Human Development and the Quest for Meaning*. New York: HarperCollins.

Francis, Leslie J., and Mandy Robbins. 2008. "Psychological Type and Prayer Preferences: A Study among Anglican Clergy in the United Kingdom." *Mental Health, Religion, and Culture* 11(1): 67–84.

Frankl, Viktor E. 1959. *Man's Search for Meaning: An Introduction to Logotherapy*. Boston: Beacon Press.

Fuller, Robert C. 2006. *Wonder: from Emotion to Spirituality*. Chapel Hill: The University of North Carolina Press.

Gardner, Howard 1993, *Multiple Intelligences, The Theory in Practice*, Basic Books.

Goleman, Daniel. 1995. *Emotional Intelligence: Why It Can Matter More Than IQ*. New York: Bantam Books.

Goliszek, Andrew. 2003. *In the Name of Science: A History of Secret Programs, Medical Research, and Human Experimentation*. New York: Saint Martin's Press.

Gordon, Howard Gardner Lynn Melby. 2006. "Gardner, Howard (1943–)." *Encyclopedia of Human Development, Volume 2*. Edited by Neil J. Salkind. Thousand Oaks, CA: SAGE Reference. Gale Virtual Reference Library. Accessed October 27, 2014.

Hannam, James. 2011. *The Genesis of Science, How the Christian Middle Ages Launched the Scientific Revolution*. London: Icon Books Ltd.

Haught, John F. 2012. *Science and Faith: A New Introduction*. New York: Paulist Press.

Haviland, William A. 1987. *Cultural Anthropology*, 5th ed. New York: Holt Rhinehart Winston.

Hoffman, E. 1992. *Psychology Today* Magazine, Jan 1992, *Overcoming Evil: An Interview with Abraham Maslow, Founder of Humanistic Psychology*.

Huntley, H. E. 1970. *The Divine Proportion: A Study in Mathematical Beauty*. Mineola, NY: Dover Publications.

Huxley, Thomas Henry 1860, Letter to Charles Kingsley

James, William. 1907. *Pragmatism: A New Name for Some Old Ways of Thinking*. New York: Longman's, Green and Company.

James, William. 1902. *The Varieties of Religious Experiences*. London: Longman Publishing Group.

Jung, Carl G., Marie-Louise Von Franz, Joseph L. Henderson, Jolande Jacobi, and Aniela Jaffe. 1964. *Man and His Symbols*. New York: Ferguson Publishing.

Keirsey, David, and Marilyn Bates. 1984. *Please Understand Me: Character and Temperament Types*. Del Mar, CA: Prometheus Nemesis Books.

Kelsey, Morton 1980, *Adventure Inward, Christian Growth through Personal Journal Writing*, Augsburg Publishing House.

Kidder, Tracy. 1981. *The Soul of a New Machine*. New York: Little Brown.

Knuth, Donald E. 2001. *Things a Computer Scientist Rarely Talks About*. Stanford, CA: CSLI Publications.

Lindberg, David C. 1992. *The Beginnings of Western Science, The European Scientific Tradition in Philosophical, Religious, and Institutional Context, 600 BC to AD 1450*. Chicago: University of Chicago Press.

Luft, Joseph, and Harry Ingham. 1955. "The Johari Window: A Graphic Model of Interpersonal Awareness." Proceedings of the Western Training Laboratory in Group Development, UCLA, Los Angeles, CA.

Maslow, Abraham H. 1966. *The Psychology of Science: A Reconnaissance*. Washington, DC: Henry Regnery Company.

Maslow, Abraham H. 1968. *Toward a Psychology of Being*. Washington, DC: Van Nostrand Reinhold Publishing.

Matsakis, Aphrodite. 1992. *I Can't Get Over It: A Handbook for Trauma Survivors*. Oakland, CA: New Harbinger Publications.

Mattoon, Mary Ann, 1981. *Jungian Psychology in Perspective,* Free Press.

McKay, Matthew, Martha Davis, and Patrick Fanning. 1995. *How to Communicate*, 2nd ed. Lyndhurst, NJ: Barnes & Noble Books.

McKay, Matthew, Peter D. Rogers, and Judith McKay. 1989. *When Anger Hurts: Quieting the Storm Within*. Oakland, CA: New Harbinger Publications, Inc.

Michael, Chester P., and Marie C. Norrisey. 1984. *Prayer and Temperament: Different Prayer Forms for Different Personality Types.* Charlottesville, VA: The Open Door, Inc.

Oatley, Keith, and Jennifer M. Jenkins. 1996. *Understanding Emotions.* Malden: MA: Blackwell Publishers.

O'Connor, Peter. 1985. *Understanding Jung, Understanding Yourself.* New York: Paulist Press.

Paintner, Christine Valters. 2011. *Lectio Divina—The Sacred Art: Transforming Words and Images into Heart-Centered Prayer.* Woodstock, VT: Skylight Paths Publishing.

Peck, M. Scott.1978. *The Road Less Traveled: A New Psychology of Love, Traditional Values and Spiritual Growth.* New York: Simon and Schuster, 173.

Perrine, Laurence, and Thomas R. Arp. 1993. *Literature: Structure, Sound and Sense*, 6th ed. San Diego, CA: Harcourt.

Phillips, J. B. 1952. *Your God is Too Small.* London: MacMillan Publishing.

Piaget, Jean. 1964. *The Early Growth of Logic in the Child.* London: Routledge and Kegan Paul.

Pine, Ronald C. 1988. *Science and the Human Prospect.* Belmont, CA: Wadsworth Publishing Company.

Poincaré, Henrí. 2007. *Science and Method.* Translated by Francis Maitland. New York: Dover.

Powell, John. 1969. *Why Am I Afraid to Tell You Who I Am?* Boston: Argus Communications.

Principe, Lawrence M. 2011. *The Scientific Revolution: A Very Short Introduction*. Oxford: Oxford University Press.

Rogers, Carl R. 1961. *On Becoming a Person: A Therapist's View of Psychotherapy*. New York: Houghton Mifflin Company.

Sacks, Rabbi Jonathan 2011. *The Great Partnership: Science, Religion, and the Search for Meaning*. New York: Schocken Books, 97.

Samovar, Larry A., and Richard E. Porter. 2000. *Intercultural Communication: A Reader*, 9th ed. Boston: Wadsworth Cengage Learning.

Sandelands, Lloyd, and Arne Carlsen. 2013. "Wonder Divine, At End but Ever New." *Theology and Science* 11(3): 304 ff.

Schmidt, Richard H. 2008. *God Seekers: Twenty Centuries of Christian Spiritualties*. Grand Rapids, MI: Wm. B. Eerdmans Publishing Company.

Shea, William R., and Mariano Artiga 2003. *Galileo in Rome: The Rise and Fall of a Troublesome Genius*. New York: Oxford 06. *Sacred Geometry: Deciphering the Code*. New York: Sterling Publishing.

Smethurst, Arthur F. 1976. *Modern Science and Christian Beliefs*. Nashville, TN: Abingdon Press.

Spinoza, Baruch 1985. *The Collected Works of Spinoza*. Edited and Translated by Edwin M. Curley. Princeton, NJ: Princeton University Press.

Tagore, Rabindranath 2007. *The English Writings of Rabindranath Tagore*. New Delhi: Atlantic Publishers and Distributors.

Tarnas, Richard 1991. *The Passion of the Western Mind: Understanding the Ideas That Have Shaped Our World View*. New York: Crown Publishing.

Taylor, Daniel. 1995. *The Healing Power of Stories: Creating Yourself through the Stories of Your Life*. New York: Doubleday.

Thorndike, Edward 1920. "A Constant Error in Psychological Ratings." *Journal of Applied Psychology* 4(1): 25–9.

Townes, Charles H. IBM THINK, Vol. 32, No. 2.

Townes, Charles. 2013. *Theology and Science* 11(3):185.

Turkle, Sherry. 1984. *The Second Self: Computers and the Human Spirit*. New York: Simon and Schuster.

Ulrich's Periodicals Directory, R. R. Bowker, 2001.

Webster's Seventh New Collegiate Dictionary. 1967. Springfield, MA: G. & C. Merriam Company.

Wikipedia, The Free Encyclopedia, s.v. "Dandelion," https://en.wikipedia.org/wiki/Taraxacum.

Wikipedia, The Free Encyclopedia, s.v. "Silicon," https://en.wikipedia.org/wiki/Silicon.

Wilber, Ken, ed. 2001. *Quantum Questions: Mystical Writings of the World's Greatest Physicists*. Boston: Shambhala Publications, Inc.

Wilczek, Frank. 2015. *A Beautiful Question: Finding Nature's Deep Design*. New York: Viking.

Yanofsky, Noson S. 2013. *The Outer Limits of Reason: What Science, Mathematics, and Logic Cannot Tell Us*. Cambridge, MA: The MIT Press.

INDEX

Illustration Credits

Front Cover

"Chambered Nautilus Shell" by Jitze Couperus, Flickr, Creative Commons.

Chapter 1 The Scientific Revolution: Uncovering the Beauty

Fig. 1-Planetary orbits: Young, Charles Augustus. 1915. *The Elements of Astronomy: A Textbook*. 1919. Andesite Press, p. 223. Flickr Creative Commons. No known copyright restrictions.

Fig. 2.-Nicolas Copernicus, "Woodcut by Tobias Stimmer, 16th Century," by Margaret Maloney, Flickr Creative Commons.

Fig. 3.-Johannes Kepler: "Bildnis des Ioannes Keplerus," from Leipzig University Library, 2015, Public Domain Mark 1.0.

Fig.4.-Galileo: Fondo Antiguo de la Biblioteca de Sevilla, Historia universal/por Cesar Cantu; trducida del italiano con arreglo a la 7a ed. De Turin, anotada por Nemesio Fernadez Cuesta, Madrid, Imprenta de Gaspar y Roig, 1854–1859, Flickr Creative Commons.

Fig 5.-Isaac Newton: "Bildnis des Isaac Newton." From Leipzig University Library, 2015, Public Domain Mark 1.0.

Fig 6.-Mechanical clockwork: "Pocket Watch" by Jeffrey Smith, Flickr Creative Commons.

Chapter 2 Important Differences in Languages
Fig 7.-Levels of Knowing: "Mist at CAT" by Paul Williams, Centre for Alternative Technology, Flickr Creative Commons.

Chapter 3 A Common Ground
Fig 8.-Common roots: Photograph by author

Fig 9.-Rachel Carson: "Rachel Carson" by Orionpozo, Flickr Creative Commons.

Fig 10.-Dandelion: "Helping Nature Along" by James Jordan, Flickr Creative Commons.

Fig 11.-Thomas A. Edison [front]: Nineteenth-Century American Trade Cards Collection, Boston Public Library, Print Department, Flickr Creative Commons.

Chapter 4 Some Limitations of Science

Chapter 5 What Does It Mean to Be Human?

Fig 12.-Viktor E. Frankel: "Viktor Frankl" by Dr. Franz Vesely, Flickr Creative Commons.

Fig 13.-Growth rings: "Annual Rings" by Christian Schettelker, Flickr Creative Commons.

Fig 14.-Russian nesting dolls: "Manushka" by S. Faric, Flickr Creative Commons.
Fig 15.-Knots: Photograph by Ruby.

Chapter 6 Our Emotions: Friends or Enemies?
Fig 16.-ABC theory: Graphics by Mark Hamer

Chapter 7 Achieving Deep, Quality Relations with Others
Fig 17.-Martin Buber: "Martin Buber" by Tullio Saba, HUO55542, Public Domain Mark 1.0.

Chapter 8 Moving Forward, Obstacles to Overcome
Fig 18.-USB connector: "USB Connector" by Liam Dunn, Flickr Creative Commons.
Fig 19.- "Carl Jung for Pifal" by Arturo Espinosa, Flickr Creative Commons.

Back cover
"Tide Comes In," by Richard, Fort Clonque, Alderney, Flicker Creative Commons.
Author photograph, by Life Touch Studios.

68362605R00148

Made in the USA
San Bernardino, CA
02 February 2018